THE HISTORY

OF

SAINT AUGUSTINE, FLORIDA

WITH

AN INTRODUCTORY ACCOUNT OF THE EARLY SPANISH
AND FRENCH ATTEMPTS AT EXPLORATION
AND SETTLEMENT IN THE TERRI-
TORY OF FLORIDA

TOGETHER WITH

SKETCHES OF EVENTS AND OBJECTS OF INTEREST CONNECTED WITH THE
OLDEST TOWN IN THE UNITED STATES

TO WHICH IS ADDED

A SHORT DESCRIPTION OF THE CLIMATE AND
ADVANTAGES OF SAINT AUGUSTINE
AS A HEALTH RESORT

BY

WILLIAM. W. DEWHURST

NEW YORK
G. P. PUTNAM'S SONS
182 FIFTH AVENUE
1881

Notice

In many older books, foxing (or discoloration) occurs and, in some instances, print lightens with wear and age. Reprinted books, such as this, often duplicate these flaws, notwithstanding efforts to reduce or eliminate them. The pages of this reprint have been digitally enhanced and, where possible, the flaws eliminated in order to provide clarity of content and a pleasant reading experience.

Copyright © 1881, William W. Dewhurst

Originally Published
New York: 1881

Reprinted by:

Janaway Publishing, Inc.
732 Kelsey Ct.
Santa Maria, California 93454
(805) 925-1038
www.janawaygenealogy.com

2013

ISBN: 978-1-59641-299-6

Made in the United States of America

PREFACE.

This brief outline of the history of one of the most interesting portions of our country, together with the sketches of the celebrated characters and memorable events which have rendered the town of St. Augustine famous throughout the world, is offered to the public in the hope and expectation that the information herein contained may supply the desire, felt by an ever-increasing number of its citizens and visitors, to be better informed as to the early history of a place so justly celebrated.

The desire of the author has been to condense and render accessible to the general reader the very interesting but elaborate accounts of the early writers concerning some of the more notable events connected with the early settlement and defense of St. Augustine.

Copious quotations have been borrowed, and the quaint language of the early historians has been retained as peculiarly appropriate to the subject and locality described.

The traditions and chronicles in possession of the descendants of the early settlers have been sought with a desire to preserve these fragments of history before it shall be too late. Already those conversant with the events of the early years of the century have passed from the stage of life.

PREFACE.

The reader who desires to become better informed as to the events noticed in this volume should consult the narrative of De Soto, by a Knight of Elvas, the works of Cabeça de Vaca, Garcilasa de la Vega, Laudonnère, Bartram, Romans, Vignoles, Roberts, De Brahm, Stork, Forbes, Darby, Williams, and Fairbanks, to all of whom the author is under obligation.

ST. AUGUSTINE, FLORIDA, *November*, 1880.

CONTENTS.

CHAPTER I.
Introductory.. 1

CHAPTER II.
The Discovery of Florida.. 3

CHAPTER III.
Expeditions of Muruelo, Cordova, Alminos, Ayllon, and Narvaez.... 7

CHAPTER IV.
Hernando De Soto.—An Account of his March through Florida....... 18

CHAPTER V.
Huguenot Settlement under Ribault.............................. 26

CHAPTER VI.
Second Huguenot Settlement under Laudonnère 29

CHAPTER VII.
The Unfortunate Expedition under Ribault.—Founding of St. Augustine by Menendez, 1565.—Attack upon the French Settlement on the St. Johns River.. 37

CHAPTER VIII.
Shipwreck of Ribault's Fleet.—Massacre by Menendez.............. 46

CHAPTER IX.
Expedition and Retaliation of De Gourges....................... 57

CHAPTER X.
Return of Menendez.—Attempt to Christianize the Indians.—Attack upon St. Augustine by Sir Francis Drake.—Murder of the Friars.. 66

CONTENTS.

CHAPTER XI.

Plunder of the Town by Captain Davis.—Removal of the Yemassee Indians.—Construction of the Fort.—Building of the First Seawall.—Attacks of Governor Moore and Colonel Palmer............ 79

CHAPTER XII.

Oglethorpe's Attack.—Bombardment of the Fort and Town.—Capture of the Highlanders at Fort Mosa.—Old Fort at Matanzas.—Monteano's Invasion of Georgia.................................. 89

CHAPTER XIII.

The Town when delivered to the English.—Fort San Juan De Pinos.—St. Augustine as described by the English Writers in 1765 to 1775. 100

CHAPTER XIV.

The Settlement of New Smyrna by the Ancestors of a Majority of the Present Population of St. Augustine.—The Hardships endured by these Minorcan and Greek Colonists.—Their Removal to St. Augustine under the Protection of the English Governor............ 113

CHAPTER XV.

Administration of Lieut.-Governor Moultrie.—Demand of the People for the Rights of Englishmen.—Governor Tonyn burning the Effigies of Adams and Hancock.—Colonial Insurgents confined in the Fort.—Assembling of the First Legislature.—Commerce of St. Augustine under the English.—Recession of the Province to Spain... 122

CHAPTER XVI.

Return of the Spaniards.—Completion of the Cathedral.—The Oldest Church Bell in America.—The Governor's Desire to People the Province with Irish Catholics.—Some Official Orders exhibiting the Customs of the Spaniards.—Unjustifiable Interference of the United States, during the " Patriot War."—Florida an Unprofitable Possession.—Erection of the Monument to the Spanish Constitution.. 129

CHAPTER XVII.

Florida Ceded to the United States.—Attempt of the Spanish Governor to carry away the Records.—Description of St. Augustine when Transferred.—Population in 1830.—Town during the Indian War.—Osceola and Coa-cou-che.—A True Account of the Dungeon in the Old Fort, and the Iron Cages.—The Indians brought to St. Augustine in 1875.. 143

CHAPTER XVIII.

St. Augustine as it used to be.—Customs.—The Oldest Structure in the United States.—Present Population.—Objects of Interest.—Buildings Ancient and Modern.—St. Augustine during the Rebellion.—Climate.—Advantages as a Health Resort...................... 161

HISTORY OF ST. AUGUSTINE.

CHAPTER I.

INTRODUCTORY.

A UNIVERSAL desire exists to learn the origin and history of our ancestors. Even before the art of writing was perfected, bards perpetuated the traditions of the early races of men by recitations of mingled facts and fables at the periodical assemblies. These peripatetics were ever welcomed and supported by the people, and doubtless preserved many of the facts of history.

Unfortunately, among the Spanish knights, who at various times essayed the conquest of Florida, few were found to desert the shrine of Mars for that of Clio. While there are several valuable accounts of the Spanish occupation, the scope of the histories is narrow and unreliable on many most interesting subjects, and on others of no importance they are often most diffuse. Owing to the vicissitudes of the occupation of St. Augustine, there are few traditions. It is possible that the Spanish antiquarian may at some future day develop a rich mine of history in searching the ancient archives of that nation and of the Catholic Church. Valuable acquisitions have been made in this field of literature by the labors of the learned and genial Buckingham Smith, a resident of St. Augustine.

Two impulses prompted the early Spanish explorers in Florida. The first was a hope of finding gold, as it had been found in Mexico and South America. A second and probably more ostensible motive, was the desire and hope of extending the Catholic faith among the inhabitants of the New World.

The result of all their hardships and labors has proved so barren that even in our day it is impossible to contemplate the slaughters and disappointments of the brave men who invaded and who defended these ancient homes, without a pang of regret.

[1492-1498.]
CHAPTER II.

THE DISCOVERY OF FLORIDA.

The honor of having discovered Florida has been assigned by different writers to Columbus, Cabot, and De Leon.

In 1492, Columbus terminated his venturesome voyage across the Atlantic by landing at the island of St. Salvador, so called by the great Genoese explorer in remembrance of his salvation. It is said that from this island his people, on his return from Europe, ventured with him to the shores of Florida, being impressed, as were the Aborigines, with a belief that the continent possessed waters calculated to invigorate and perpetuate youth and vitality.

The date 1497 is assigned as the year in which Amerigo Vespucci discovered the western continent. Vespucci was encouraged by Emanuel, King of Portugal, and, though probably lacking the inspiring genius and sublime courage of Columbus, through the accident of fortune he has perpetuated his name in the designation of half a hemisphere. Doubtless, Vespucci was the first to reach the mainland of the western continent, as Columbus did not touch the mainland until his third voyage in 1498, when he landed at the mouth of the Orinoco in South America. So entirely unsuspicious was the world at this time of a second continent, that the transcendent genius of Columbus never suspected the magnitude of his discovery, and he died in the belief that he had landed on the eastern shore of Asia.

The next to essay a voyage to the New World was also a native of Southern Europe. John Cabot, the son of Giovanni Gabota, a native of Venice, who had settled in Bristol, was commissioned by Henry the Seventh of England to sail on a voyage of discovery and conquest. Though the inception and authority for the expedition antedated the sailing of Columbus by a year, Cabot did not leave England until May, 1498. His landing on America was at or near the river St. Lawrence, from whence he sailed southward along the coast, landing only for observation, and making no attempt to form a settlement. It is doubtful if Cabot ever sailed as far south as Florida, though it is claimed that to him belongs the honor of its discovery.

Fourteen years afterward, the first landing was made on the sandy shores of Florida, and possession claimed in the name of the King of Spain.

The mystic fountain of youth, first pictured in the days of mythology, whose waters would stay the devastating march of time, endow perpetual youth, even restore vigor to the decrepitude of age, was said to exist in the New World.

This fable, with which the European had become familiar from an Egyptian or Hellenic source, found confirmation in the traditions of the Indians of the Caribbean Islands. To the mind of the Spanish knight, eager to continue his youthful prowess and the enjoyment of the adjuncts of power and authority already achieved, the belief, thus strengthened by concurrence of a tradition in the New World, seemed an authentic reality, and the sufficient foundation for great labor and sacrifice.

In this materialistic age we may laugh at the credulousness of the Spanish chevalier, whose faith in the story of an Indian girl led him to expend his wealth and sacrifice his life in such a chimerical search; yet the history of our own day will recount equal faith and as fruitless ventures.

Juan Ponce de Leon seems to have been a person of influence in Spain, possessed of a unique character, a chivalrous nature, and a comprehensive and trained mind. Born in an age when personal valor and knightly habits were the surest paths to distinction and authority, his career seems to have been that of an adventurer. When past the meridian of life, he landed in the Bahamas seeking for the spring of youth. In vain was his search, but his hopes and his ardor were undaunted. "Upon the mainland the wished-for waters flowed as a river, on whose banks lived the rejuvenated races in serene idleness and untold luxuriance." Leaving the Bahamas he steered northwest for the coast. While some accounts make his first landing at a spot north of St. Augustine, it is more probable that his course was to the west of the Bahama Islands, and that he first disembarked at or near the southernmost part of Florida, at a place called Punta Tanchi, now Cape Sable.

It was on March 27th, 1512, Palm Sunday (Pasqua Florida), and from this accidental date of discovery did the country receive its name, and not from its abundance of flowers. While the Latin adjective *floridus* signifies "full of flowers," soldiers of fortune like De Leon did not make a practice of using the Latin tongue except in their litany. After erecting a cross, celebrating a solemn mass, and proclaiming the sovereignty of the Spanish crown, De Leon coasted along the Florida shore into the Gulf of Mexico, making various attempts to penetrate the interior of the country. In this he was unable to succeed, owing to the swampy nature of the land, and its barrenness of food products. After the loss of many of his men, the rest, greatly suffering for food, re-embarked.

According to some historians De Leon returned to Spain, and demanded to be made governor of the new dominions; while others declare that he withdrew only to the islands, from whence he sent a description of the newly-discovered province, and begged a grant of the same. His request was acceded to by the Spanish crown on condition that he should colonize the country.

Accordingly, in 1516 he returned with two vessels, but his occupancy being disputed by the Indians, De Leon was mortally wounded in the first encounter. His followers, being dispirited by the loss of their leader in a strange and uninviting land, returned on board their vessels and sailed for Cuba. Here a monument was erected to the memory of Juan Ponce de Leon, on which is inscribed the following eloquent and deserved epitaph: "Mole sub hac, fortis requiescunt, ossa Leonis qui vicit factis nomina magna suis."

Though De Leon died in disappointment, never having tasted the fabled waters of which he came in search, his name will ever be associated with the country he christened, and many a wasted consumptive who has regained a lost vigor and health under the assuasive influences of Florida's climate will give a kindly thought of remembrance and regret as he recalls him who first visited Florida, a seeker after healing waters.

[1517.]
CHAPTER III.

EXPEDITIONS OF MURUELO, CORDOVA, ALMINOS, AYLLON, AND NARVAEZ.

In the next twenty years there were many captains who undertook voyages for the exploration and subjugation of Florida.

It must be remembered that at this time, and until the beginning of the eighteenth century, the grand divisions of North America were known only as Florida and Canada.

Diego Muruelo, a Spanish adventurer, by profession a pilot, is said to have sailed from Cuba, and returning with gold and precious stones obtained from the Florida Indians, spread glowing reports of the country. These reports may have influenced the home government, as about this time a Dominican, "Bernardo de Mesa," was chosen Bishop of Cuba "including Florida."

Fernandez de Cordova landed on the coast, but was driven off by the Indians, and returned to Cuba, where he died of his wounds. The famous Bernal Diaz was a member of this expedition.

One De Alminos, a member of Cordova's party, made such a favorable report of the country and the advantages to be derived from a possession of the same that he induced Francisco de Geray, the governor of Jamaica, to furnish him with three vessels, with which he returned to the coast; but was unsuccessful in his attempts to make any acquisition of wealth or power in Florida, though slight progress was made in the survey of its coast. De Geray, however, trusting in the reports given him, applied to the home government to be made Adelantado of Florida, though his request is said to have been denied.

Lucas Vasquez de Ayllon, an auditor of St. Domingo, a rich and learned man, formed a company with six other inhabitants of the island of Hispaniola, for the purpose of securing Indians to work as slaves in the mines of Mexico.

In the humane laws decreed by the Spanish crown against the enslaving of its Indian subjects, an exception had been made against the Caribs, or Cannibals; these Indians being considered especially barbarous and deserving of castigation.

De Ayllon falsely declaring that the inhabitants of the mainland were Caribs, set sail in 1520 with two vessels, and directed his course to the east coast of Florida. He landed in the province of Chicora in South Carolina, where the Indians were ruled by a chief named Datha who was a giant. His gigantic stature had been attained by a process of stretching which elongated the bones while a child. This practice was applied only to those of royal race.

The simple Floridians at first fled from the vessels and their pale-faced occupants. The Spaniards, however, by kind treatment succeeded in assuring the Indians, and, finally, induced the cacique and a hundred and thirty attendants on board the ships. These were at once secured, and the ships set sail for Hispaniola. It is also said that, as a parting salute, De Ayllon fired the cannon of the ships into the crowd assembled on the shores; but this inhuman act is not authenticated, and the treachery of which he certainly was guilty is sufficiently execrable to account for that remorse which he is said to have suffered afterward. One vessel was lost on the voyage, and the cargo of the other was sold upon their arrival at St. Domingo. The North American Indians, however, have never submitted like the African to the servile yoke. The Christianizing and civilizing blessings of slavery have never been appreciated by these Indians. This body of North American captives, the first which history mentions, set an example which has been followed by their unfortunate descendants. No promises nor hopes could influence these to forget their heritage of freedom. Refusing all sustenance, borne down by sorrow and home-sickness, to a man they chose death rather than slavery.

Charles the Fifth had been so affected by the eloquent and earnest appeals of that humane and nobly pious Bishop of Chiapa, Bartholomi de las Casas, that he issued decrees visiting his anger and the severest penalties upon the Spanish governors who, by their barbarous tyranny, had made the Indians of the New World to detest Christianity, and tremble at the very name of Christian. Though these ordinances appear often to have been disregarded, Vasquez's perfidious treatment of the natives seems to have been disapproved at Court ; for when he applied to the Spanish Crown for the governorship of the province, his request was granted on condition that he should not enslave the Indians.

Tempted by the profit of his first venture, he disregarded this provision of his grant, and returned to secure a second cargo. The Indians were equal to the occasion, and met the whites with their own methods. Having decoyed the Spaniards away from the shore, the Indians fell upon them and killed two hundred. The Spaniards after this attack put to sea, and soon after encountering a severe storm were shipwrecked, and are all reported to have perished except Vasquez himself, who was picked up and saved, only to pass the remainder of his life in misery and remorse. His unhappiness may have had for its cause his disgrace and the displeasure of the king, which he is said to have incurred. Another account says he was among the killed.

Despising the ignorant and untrained races of Indians and overweeningly confident in the mighty influence of the name of his king and the power of the Spanish arms, Pamphilo de Narvaez, having obtained from Charles the Fifth a grant of all the lands from Cape Florida to the River of Palms in Mexico, determined to extend the Spanish rule and the Catholic faith. Narvaez was also actuated by a desire to retrieve his own disgrace. Having been sent to Mexico by Valasquez, the Governor of Cuba, to supersede Cortez, the latter had by a sudden attack seized Narvaez and assumed the command of his forces, who were doubtless only too willing to serve under so gallant and successful a commander.

Returning to Spain, Narvaez was unable to obtain redress for the injuries sustained at the hands of Cortez, but was placated by the Commission of Adelantado of Florida.

On the 12th day of April, 1528, he sailed from St. Jago de Cuba, with four hundred men and forty horses. Landing near what is now Charlotte Harbor, he took formal possession of the country in the name of the King of Spain.

The houses of the Indians, already evacuated, were in sight of the bay. Proceeding inland, he came upon a town located on another and larger bay (Tampa Bay), where the Indians offered him corn.

Here was promulgated a manifesto prepared by Narvaez, in the Spanish language, abounding in arrogant assumption of power and superiority, intended to awe the Indians, and secure at once their allegiance and homage.

This curious document is still extant among the Archives of the Seville Chamber of Commerce. The proclamation throws such a light upon the estimate which the Spaniards had of the rights and condition of the Indians, of their own authority, its source, and the purposes for which it was to be exercised, that a considerable extract is quoted.

"A summons to be made to the inhabitants of the countries which extend between the River of Palms and Cape Florida:

"In the name of his Catholic and Imperial Majesty, ever august King, and Emperor of all the Romans; in the name of Dona Juana, his mother; King of Spain; Defender of the Church, always victorious, and always invincible, the conqueror of barbarous nations; I, Pamphilo de Narvaez, their servant, and Ambassador and Captain, cause to be known to you in the best manner I am able." How God created the world and charged St. Peter to be sovereign of all men in whatever country they might be born, God gave him the whole world for his inheritance. One of his successors made a gift of all these lands to the Imperial Sovereigns, the King and Queen of Spain, so that the Indians are their subjects. After claiming their allegiance he closes with the following invitation to embrace the Catholic faith, which is more after the pagan than Christian order:

"You will not be compelled to accept Christianity, but when you shall be well informed of the truth you will be made Christians. If you refuse, and delay agreeing to what I have proposed to you, I testify to you that, with God's assistance, I will march against you, arms in hand. I will make war upon you from all sides, and by every possible means. I will subject you to the yoke and obedience of the Church and His Majesty. I will obtain possession of your wives and children; I will reduce you to slavery. I notify you that neither His Majesty, nor myself, nor the gentlemen who accompany me will be the cause of this, but yourselves only." That the Indians gave little heed to the claims and threats of this haughty knight is evident from the sad result of his expedition. While resting at the village about Tampa, Narvaez was shown some wooden burial cases, containing the remains of chiefs, and ornamented with deerskins elaborately painted and adorned with sprigs of gold. Learning that the gold came from farther north, at a place called Appalache, Narvaez immediately ordered his men to march thither. With more judgment or prophetic wisdom his treasurer, Cabeca de Vaca, endeavored in vain to dissuade him. Having distributed a small quantity of biscuit and pork as rations, he set out on the 1st of May with three hundred men and forty horses. They marched through a desolate country, crossing one large river and meeting only one settlement of Indians until the 17th of June, when they fell in with a settlement, where they were well received and supplied with corn and venison. The Spaniards learning that this tribe were enemies of the Appalacheans, exchanged presents and obtained guides to direct them to the Appalachean town. This they reached on the 25th, after a fatiguing march through swamps and marshes, and at once attacked the inhabitants without warning, and put them all to the sword.

The town consisted of comfortable houses well stocked with corn, skins, and garments made from bark cloth. Not finding the wealth he had expected, and being subject to the repeated attacks of the Indians, Narvaez, after a month's rest at Appalache, divided his command into three companies, and ordered them to scour the country.

These companies returning, after an unsuccessful search for

gold or food, the Spaniards continued their march toward the north and west, carrying with them in chains the Indian chief captured at Appalache. This plan of securing the chief of an Indian nation or tribe, and forcing him to march with the troops as a guide and hostage, seems to have been adopted by each of the Spanish commanders, and always with disastrous results. The sight of an Indian chief in chains aroused a feeling of outraged friendship wherever they passed, and gave a premonition of the servile fate that would be assigned to their race whenever the Spaniards obtained the dominion. This captive urged on the Indians to harass and persistently follow up the marching army, influencing even tribes that were inimical to himself.

The march of Narvaez through the western part of Florida continued until fall, with an unvarying succession of attacks and skirmishes at every halt, and often pitched battles at the towns that lay in his path. Little progress was made on their journey, owing to the uncertainty of their course, the unproductive and difficult nature of the country traversed, and the unremitting attacks and obstacles opposed by the wily Indians, who were ever on the watch to pick off man or beast, and prevent the collection of supplies.

Disheartened at the continued losses sustained by his army, and despairing of ever reaching by land the Spanish settlements in Mexico, Narvaez, having reached the banks of a large river, determined to follow it to its mouth, and take to the sea.

Slowly they moved down the river, and arrived at its mouth in a sadly distressed condition. Despair lent them an energy that was fanned to a burning zeal by the hopes of being able to reach their friends and salvation on the shores of the same waters before their view. A smith in their party declared that he could build a forge, and with bellows made of hides, and the charcoal they could supply abundantly, he forged from their swords and accoutrements bolts and nails for building boats.

Diligently they worked, incited by the memory of all their hardships and perils, and the joyous hope of safe delivery. Such was their energy and determination, that in six weeks they constructed from the material at hand, five large boats capable of holding fifty men each. For cordage they twisted ropes from the manes and tails of their horses, together with the fiber of plants; their sails were made from their clothing, and from the hides of their horses they made sacks to hold water.

With these frail and clumsily constructed crafts, open boats loaded almost to the water's edge, and without a navigator in the party, or provisions for a single week did this little army of desperate men set out on the open sea. Narvaez commanded one boat. The others were under the command of his captains, one of whom, Cabeça de Vaca, has preserved to us the account of this fatal expedition.

De Vaca gives a long and minute account of their voyage, and the hardships and misfortunes they underwent until they were all shipwrecked, and out of the two hundred and forty who started on the return only fifteen were alive. Narvaez himself was blown off from the shore while almost alone in his boat and never again heard of. Only these four are known certainly to have been saved, Cabeca de Vaca, the treasurer of the expedition, Captain Alonzo Castillo, Captain Andreas Orantes, and a negro or Turk, named Estevanico.

These managed to preserve their lives, and attain an influence among the Indians by pretending to a knowledge of physic, and a supernatural origin. Their method of practice was unique, and as universal in its application to every form of disease as that of the celebrated Dr. Sangrado. It consisted in marking the patient with the sign of the cross, repeating over him a paternoster or Ave Maria, and then calling upon him to assure his comrades that he was entirely healed. The fee for this skillful treatment was the customary reward among the Indians for the services of the Medicine Man, the transfer of all the worldly possessions of the patient to the physician in exchange for restored health. The Indians thus despoiled by Cabeça de Vaca and his companions begged them not to be distressed about it, assuring them that they held the loss of their goods as naught in comparison with the pleasure of having beheld the children of the sun, who had the power to heal the sick and take away life. They declared they should hide nothing from them, because everything was known to these divinities. So great was the terror which their presence inspired, that for the first few days upon their arrival in any new place, the inhabitants never stood before them without trembling, and did not dare to speak nor lift up their eyes. De Vaca says : "We kept up much state and gravity with them, and in order to maintain this we spoke but seldom to them. The negro who was with us talked often to them, informed himself of the roads we wished to take, of the villages we should come upon, and of other things which we desired to know. Although we knew six languages we could not in all parts make use of them, as we found more than a thousand different languages. If we had had an interpreter so that we could have made ourselves perfectly understood we should have left them all Christians." *

---

* Naufragios de Alvar Nuñez Cabeça de Vaca, cap. 31. Barcia, Historiadores, tom. ii.

Thus did Cabeça de Vaca and his companions for nearly six years pursue their journey among the Indians. During all this long period they never once abandoned their hope and design of reaching Mexico. Finally after many other strange adventures De Vaca arrived at the Spanish settlements in Mexico, and was received by his countrymen with the greatest consideration and rejoicing.

Having been sent over to Spain, he presented to the crown a narrative of the unfortunate expedition of Narvaez, representing that the country contained great wealth that he alone was able to secure, and begging that he be made the governor. In this he was disappointed, however, but was placated by the government of La Plata, in South America. The narrative of De Vaca has been received by historians and antiquarians as in the main veracious, though describing some wonderful customs and people. It is the earliest account of Florida which we possess, having been published in 1555, and is of inestimable value.

Among the sailors in the ill-starred expedition of Narvaez was one Juan Ortiz, who has attained a celebrity on account of his connection with the later expedition of De Soto. Ortiz was among those who returned to Cuba at the beginning of the expedition. It is said that the wife of Narvaez, by a great reward, induced him to accept the command of a small vessel which she fitted out to go in search of her husband. Ortiz, having returned to the shores of Florida, was decoyed by the Indians to put himself in their power, and was then seized and brought before the chief named Hiriga, or Hirrihigua, who, feeling inflamed at the treatment he had received at the hands of Narvaez, ordered the captive to be stretched out on a pile and burned to death. Then history relates an episode similar to that of Captain John Smith and Pocahontas, only more romantic. In this case not only did the beautiful Indian maiden supplicate an angry father, and clothe the quality of mercy in such attractive garb as to melt the flinty heart of a stern old savage ; but, having procured the release of Ortiz from his imminent peril, she, with her equally noble and heroic affianced husband, sacrificed their love on the altar of humanity. Ortiz having been set to watch a burying-ground, allowed a wolf to drag off the body of a lately-buried chief, and though he pursued and killed the wolf, he was again sentenced to death to appease the outraged spirit. In despair of saving a life that was so justly forfeited, the daughter of the chief sent Ortiz to her lover, a neighboring chief named Macaco, who protected him for a period of twelve years until the arrival of De Soto. He thus incurred the enmity of Hiriga, who refused to consent to the alliance with his daughter unless the white man was sacrificed to placate the wrath of the spirit he had failed to protect. Unfortunately history has failed to preserve the name of this remarkable girl, and still more unfortunate is it that there is no reason to believe that after the arrival of De Soto, any return was made the chief's daughter, which would show an appreciation by the white men of conduct so worthy of the highest encomiums and reward.

CHAPTER IV.

HERNANDO DE SOTO.—AN ACCOUNT OF HIS MARCH THROUGH FLORIDA.

MISLED by the fabulous stories told of the wealth of Florida, and by the still more deceptive innuendoes in the account of De Vaca, and having before their eyes continually the immense treasures actually secured in Peru and Mexico, the Spaniards were satisfied that it only needed a force sufficiently large and ably commanded to secure to the conquerors even greater treasures in their northern possessions. They were, moreover, convinced that the Indian tribes would not defend, with such persistent valor and great sacrifices, a worthless country, when the incalculable wealth of the Aztec had been so feebly defended.

At this favorable moment there appeared at court a man who was acknowledged to be eminently qualified to inspire confidence in any undertaking he might enter upon. No knight stood higher in the esteem of his sovereign, or enjoyed greater popularity with the cavaliers than Hernando de Soto. Born of a good family in the northern part of Spain, he had early entered the service of D'Avilas, the governor of the West Indies, by whom he was put in command of a detachment sent to Peru to reinforce Pizarro.

Here he exhibited remarkable courage and capacities, and soon rose to be second in command. Having gained a valuable experience and a splendid reputation in the conquest of Peru, he was induced by Pizarro to seek his pleasure or glory in another field, lest his own achievements should be rivaled by those of his lieutenant. A million and a half of dollars was the sum which he received on relinquishing the field. This, in those days, princely fortune was but a small portion of the exorbitant ransom paid by the captured Inca.

Returning to Spain, his wealth and achievements seem to have excited genuine admiration rather than envy, and he at once became the favorite of the court. His martial spirit craved adventures, and could not remain content with the dullness of court life. He therefore petitioned the king to be allowed to fit out an expedition to occupy and settle the Spanish northern possessions. The country at that time designated as Florida extended from the Chesapeake Bay to Mexico, and, as was thought, embraced the richest portion of the world, full of all things good.

De Soto's request having been granted, he was at once commissioned Adelantado and Marquis of Florida. A fleet of seven ships and three cutters was at once purchased, and armed and equipped for the expedition, and, as it was De Soto's intention to colonize the country, much attention was given to providing a supply of such seeds and animals as were desirable to introduce. It is possible that some of the seeds scattered by the followers of De Soto may to-day be reproducing themselves in Florida. The origin of the wild horses of America has also been assigned to the Spanish introduction at this time. So great was the desire to accompany De Soto, and so certain seemed the rich recompense of wealth and honor to be achieved under such a leader, that the complement of a thousand chosen men was recruited with ease.

Of this number more than three hundred were gentlemen of rank, knights and hidalgoes of the best blood of Spain, who lavished their means in the purchase of arms and equipments, thinking that with these they would procure wealth in plenty. With this brilliant corps were twelve priests, to minister to the spiritual welfare of the Spaniards, or Indians, or both.

Leaving Spain in the spring, the fleet proceeded as far as Cuba, where it was delayed a while in completing the arrangements. Here De Soto married the lady Isabella, a sister of the famous Bovadilla. The enjoyment of the society of his new wife, however, could not detain him from the pursuit of honor. In May, 1539, he left Cuba and landed in Florida on Whitsunday, in the same month. The bay in which they landed, now called Tampa Bay, was named by them "Espiritu Santo," in honor of the day on which they arrived. A detailed account of the march of De Soto would be too long to introduce in a work like this. There were two reports published in the sixteenth century, both of which have been translated into English. While of great value and interest, they both contain much that is fabulous and exaggerated. Soon after beginning the march northward, the advance guard of the Spaniards fell in with a body of Indians, who advanced apparently to oppose them. The Spanish captain, thinking it was an assault, ordered a charge, when, greatly to their surprise, they heard the Spanish tongue in a supplication not to kill one of their own countrymen. The speaker proved to be the captive Ortiz, before mentioned. Having acquired a knowledge of the Indian language he was a great acquisition to the command, though unable, from his restricted confinement, to give a satisfactory reply to the first question asked him by his countrymen, "Where was there any gold to be found?" By the advice of Ortiz, or from motives of policy, De Soto pursued a pacific policy at first, and met with friendly treatment and generous supplies of provisions at the various Indian towns. The Indians, at that time, seemed to have paid considerable attention to agriculture, and to have lived in towns that were rudely fortified, and built with very considerable dwelling houses and barns. Some of the houses of the chiefs are described as more than a hundred feet long, containing many rooms, and set upon artificial mounds. They were built of palings, sometimes plastered with clay, and covered with thatch. At nearly every town the Spaniards found provisions stored, consisting of walnuts, dried grapes, beans, millet, and corn, besides growing vegetables, among which are mentioned beets. Some of the towns must have been very large, as many as six thousand inhabitants dwelling in and around several mentioned. At one town called Mabila, the baggage and valuables of the Spaniards were carried within the palisades by the Indians forced to transport them. There an attack was made upon the town, and twenty-five hundred of the savages were slain. The chief and a company of natives to transport the baggage were seized at every town, unless packmen were offered voluntarily. After marching a short distance away from their homes, the women were allowed their freedom, but the men were led by a chain attached to a Spanish soldier. Arriving at a town, these bondsmen were released, and new captives taken, to be in turn exchanged further on.

In this manner did De Soto march through what is now Florida, thence north-easterly through Georgia into South Carolina, thence back to the vicinity of Pensacola.

While in South Carolina De Soto fell in with an intelligent race of Indians, whose sovereign was a woman. Here he secured a large store of pearls, nearly three hundred pounds, some of which were said to be worth their weight in gold. These, however, were all lost, together with the other valuables and the baggage, in the burning of the town Mabila.

W. Gilmore Simms, the novelist, has seized upon the fables connected with this Indian queen, in his romance of "Andres Vasconselos."

Trusting to the disingenuous tales of the Indians, and ever led on by his overweening faith in the existence of vast stores of gold, De Soto had marched on and ever further on until, consuming a year's time, he had made a complete circuit of the country, and found himself empty-handed within six days' march of Pensacola, then called Ochuse. Here he had ordered his lieutenant, Maldonado, to await his arrival with the ships he had sent back to Cuba for a supply of provisions and mining tools.

De Soto at this time exhibited that masterly force of character which had secured his former success and his great influence. Unwilling to endure the disgrace that would attach to an unsuccessful issue of the expedition, a disaster which, with the unfortunate results of former expeditions, he feared would preclude any future attempts to settle the Spanish domains in Florida, he resolved to conceal from his followers their location and the nearness of the fleet, lest, being disheartened by their want of success and worse than uncertain prospect of the future, they would refuse to continue on, and taking possession of the ships, set sail for the West Indies. He therefore forbade Ortiz to mention to the troops the arrival of Maldonado, which had been learned from the Indians. Recruiting his men and horses by a short rest, he marched on again into the unknown wilderness, and turned his back forever upon home, friends, and all

HISTORY OF ST. AUGUSTINE.   23

that makes life worth living. Still searching for gold he marched from region to region, ever meeting and overcoming difficulties and opposition, and yet unsuccessful. He proceeded as high as the Cumberland River, then turned west, crossed the Mississippi, and reached the Red River. In that region the Spaniards wintered, and in the spring De Soto retraced his steps to the Mississippi, having determined to reach the mouth of that river, from whence he could send to Mexico and Cuba for further supplies. The disappointment and mortification which his gallant nature had so long opposed was eating like a cancer into his heart, and unsustained by a hope, which in other circumstances would have thrown off disease, his body at last gave way to fatigue and malaria, and he began to sink under a wasting fever. Deep despondency settled down upon him as he thought of home, his young wife, and all the comforts and prospects he had put so far from his reach. Calling his followers about him, he thanked them for their courage and devotion, and besought them to accept of his appointment of a successor to lead them after his death, which he assured them was near at hand. His followers tried to afford him the regulation comfort at such times, depicting this life as so full of misery that he was most happy who was soonest relieved of its burden. They finally received from him the appointment of Louis Moscoza as their captain.

Shortly after, on the 21st day of May, 1542, died that chivalrous knight, Don Hernando de Soto, Governor of Cuba, and Adelantado of Florida, far from his native land, in the wilderness on the banks of that great Father of Waters, whose vast and turbid flow ever recalls his great name and deeds, and whose discovery has proved his most enduring remembrance.

Desirous of impressing the Indians with the supernatural

origin of De Soto, his followers declared that his father, the Sun God, had taken him to himself, and lest their deception should be manifested by the sight of his dead body, the corpse of their illustrious and beloved leader was placed in a canoe, and in the darkness of the night consigned to the waters of the mighty river.

Immediately after the death of De Soto, the Spaniards began to build boats and collect provisions in preparation for their long voyage. They continued thus employed until the annual floods had subsided, when they descended to the gulf. Though continuously receiving attacks from the Indians, they at last reached the Spanish settlement of Panuco, in Mexico. Here they were received with joy, and every kindness proffered them. Three hundred and eleven men kneeled before the altar in thanksgiving to God for their safe deliverance from those distresses and perils which had swept away more than two-thirds of the gallant army that four years before had landed in Florida, an army that had overrun a country containing thousands of brave inhabitants, subsisted for more than three years on the country through which it passed, ever maintained the unity of its command and devotion to its valorous leader while he lived, and executed his wishes after his death.

In 1559 the Spaniards made another attempt to explore Florida. Mendoza, the governor of Mexico, under advices from Spain, ordered the equipment of a larger and more complete expedition than ever had landed in Florida.

Fifteen hundred soldiers and many of the religious orders set sail from Vera Cruz in the spring of 1559, under the command of a soldier of some reputation, Don Tristan de Luna. Landing near Pensacola, the Spaniards underwent an experience similar to that encountered by their countrymen in the previous expeditions, and after being distressed by hunger, weakened by losses, and divided by mutiny, finally returned without having accomplished more than to view the desolation wrought by De Soto and Narvaez in the country through which they had passed.

CHAPTER V.

HUGUENOT SETTLEMENT UNDER RIBAULT.

The Spaniards having thus far been unsuccessful in making a settlement upon the shores of Florida, the country was left open to any nation which should enter upon and colonize the territory. The Admiral Gaspard de Coligni, then at the head of the Protestant party in France, perceived with the sagacity of a statesman, the advantage of a colony in America composed of French Protestants. While increasing the dominion of France, and thus gaining its promoters honor and patronage, it would afford a refuge, in case the result of the bitter contest with the Guises should prove disastrous to the Protestant party.

Charles the Ninth, then monarch of France, approved of the admiral's purpose, and furnished him with two ships. These were readily manned with zealous Huguenots, under the command of Jean Ribault, who sailed on the 18th of February, 1562, intending to enter the river Santee. Arriving on the coast in about the latitude of St. Augustine, they proceeded north, and entered a large river on the first of May, which they called the river of May. Here Ribault erected a stone monument on which was engraved the arms of France.

Continuing their exploration of the coast, they sailed north about "ninety leagues," until they finally disembarked near Port Royal, South Carolina, where they concluded to plant the colony.

The site selected for their new city was a favorable one, being in a fertile and pleasant country, "abounding in mulberry and persimmon trees, and inhabited by a race of hospitable Indians, who supplied them with food for the merest trifles." Though the prime object of the expedition had been to establish a colony in America, when the moment arrived to decide who should remain in the new settlement so far from home, and who return in the ships to France, it seems that it was necessary to appeal to the honor and the patriotism of the company to secure volunteers to retain possession of the territory which they had christened New France. Twenty-six of Ribault's followers, however, agreed to remain, under the command of Albert, one of his lieutenants.

A field, sixteen rods long and thirteen wide, was stockaded, and within this they built a fort, which they named in honor of their sovereign, Fort Charles. We shall see that this honor paid to their king was reciprocated on the part of that vacillating monarch by a total neglect of the rights and interests of his loyal subjects.

Leaving provisions and ammunition for the little colony, Ribault sailed away in the middle of July, trusting to soon return with a large company, who should be the pioneers of a great branch of the French nation on this continent. Having arrived in France, he found the government so divided by civil discord and confusion that he was unable to secure any attention for the settlement of New France.

Meanwhile Captain Albert visited the Indian chiefs in the vicinity, cultivating their friendships, and exchanging simple presents for their gifts of pearls and some silver ore, which the Indians reported as having been dug from the ground on certain high hills by a tribe who lived ten days' journey to the west.

The colonists seem to have expected to live on the provisions left within the fort until the return of the fleet from France. When the weeks passed by and their supplies began to be exhausted, with no sign of relief from France, the colonists began to be disobedient, quarrelsome, and unmanageable. In the company was one Laclerc, a licentious demagogue. This Laclerc, being opposed by Albert in his attempt to reduce certain of the Indians to slavery, raised a mutiny, in which the captain lost his life. After the death of Albert, the Indians refused to supply the colony with provisions, and their situation became so serious that they resolved to desert the country, and if possible return to France. Choosing one of their number as captain, they set to work to build a small ship and collect a store of provisions.

Having succeeded in constructing a small vessel, calked with moss and rigged with cordage made from fibrous plants, they set the sails made from their garments, and embarked to cross the wide ocean in a craft that had neither the capacity nor equipment for a coasting voyage. Soon after putting to sea they became becalmed, and continued so for twenty days, by which time they had been reduced to a starving condition.

So great was their necessity that they were about to cast lots for a victim, whose flesh should support life in the rest, when Laclerc the mutineer, offered himself as the victim. So desperate was their strait that his offer was accepted and his flesh distributed among the company. Life being sustained, they were soon after relieved from the repetition of such a shocking tragedy, being picked up by a passing vessel and taken to England. Having been brought before Queen Elizabeth, they gave such an account of Florida as to excite in her a great interest in the country.

CHAPTER VI.

SECOND HUGUENOT SETTLEMENT UNDER LAUDONNÈRE.

Coligni and the Protestants had not forgotten the forsaken colony, nor relinquished their intention of providing a refuge in America.

After two years Coligni succeeded in obtaining authority to send three ships to the succor of the colony in Florida. A company equal to the capacity of the ships quickly volunteered for the enterprise, of whom a large number belonged to families of good blood.

Having been well equipped with arms, provisions, tools, and seeds for agriculture, the fleet sailed under the command of Captain Renè Laudonnère, who had accompanied Ribault on the former expedition.

It is greatly to be regretted that the astute Coligni had not assumed in person the command of this expedition intended to establish in America a New France, forty-three years before the first settlement of the English at Jamestown, and sixty-six years before the Puritans on the *Mayflower* landed at Plymouth. His counsels would doubtless have preserved the weak colony who were so cruelly exterminated, and he himself would have escaped his untimely end. Coligni was one of the first victims of the horrid massacre of Paris on the eve of St. Bartholomew's Day, in

1572, being assassinated by one of the servants of the Duke of Guise.

Laudonnère came upon the coast at St. Augustine, but, stopping only for a reconnoisance, he sailed to the site of the former colony and Fort Charles, with the hope of relieving his countrymen. Finding the fort deserted, and learning of the time that had elapsed since the departure of the colony, he determined to return to the river May (now the St. Johns), and found his settlement on its banks, where, as he says, the "means of subsistence seemed to abound," and the signs of gold and silver observed on the former voyage had been very encouraging. These signs must have been the possession by the Indians of some pieces of quartz, which seems to have been very general, and to have led the French like the Spaniards from tribe to tribe like a very ignis-fatuus.

Laudonnère's account of his landing at the harbor of St. Augustine is extremely interesting, and by his description the location is readily recognized. He says: "We arrived on Thursday, the 22d of June (1564), about three o'clock in the afternoon, and landed at a little river which is thirty degrees distant from the equator. After we had struck sail and cast anchor athwart the river, I determined to go on shore to discover the same. Therefore, being accompanied by Mons. de Ottigni, with Mons. d'Arlac, mine Ensign, and a certain number of gentlemen and soldiers, I embarked myself about three or four o'clock in the evening, and being arrived at the mouth of the river, I caused the channel to be sounded, which was found to be very shallow, although that further within the same the water was there found reasonably deep, which separateth itself into two great arms, whereof one runneth toward the south, and the other toward the north. Having thus searched the river, I went on land to speak with the Indians, which waited for us upon the shore, which at our coming on land came before us crying with a loud voice in their Indian language 'Antipola Bonassou,' which is as much as to say, brother, friend, or some such like thing. After they had made much of us, they showed us their paracoussy, that is to say, their king or governor, to whom I presented certain toys wherewith he was well pleased and for mine own part I praised God continually for the great love I found in these savages, which were sorry for nothing but that the night approached and made us retire into our ships. Howbeit before my departure I named the river the River of Dolphins, because at mine arrival I saw there a great number of dolphins which were playing at the mouth thereof."* The dolphins or porpoises still continue to play in the river and harbor at St. Augustine, especially during the summer season. Throughout the greater part of the year rare sport could be obtained by good shots who had the skill to lodge a rifle ball in the head of the porpoise as he rises to "blow."

The Indian town located on the present site of St. Augustine was Seloy, and the same name seems to have been given to both of the rivers which unite to form the harbor. From the narration it would seem probable that the point where Laudonnère landed was upon Anastatia Island, the Indians having come over from the mainland on seeing the French ships in the offing.

Laudonnère having left Fort Charles, entered the river May, and selecting a favorable site, about six leagues distant from the mouth, built a small settlement, which he fortified with palisades

---

* Hakluyt's translation. French's Historical Collections, p. 223.

and an embankment of earth in the shape of a triangle, and named it Carolus, still doing honor to the king who so little deserved esteem. With a religious fervor characteristic of the age, and probably heightened by their isolation, and proximity to the vast ocean which they had just passed in safety, and solemnly impressed by their surroundings on a vast and unexplored continent, the little band of strangers assembled and dedicated their work and themselves to the glory of God and the advancement of his holy faith.

The site of the Huguenot settlement is now known as St. John's Bluff, the first point of high land on the south after entering the St. Johns River from the ocean. It is a sightly hill, probably formed by sand dunes at an early period when the shore was far to the west of its present coast line. The bluff rises some forty feet above the river, and is covered with a thick growth of oaks and other hard woods. At the foot of the hill on the east lay the broad marshes stretching for four or five miles toward the sea, and reaching to the narrow ridge of sands and woods adjoining the beach. The channel of the river here approaches the southern bank, and the strong current sweeping in against the mobile sands at each tide has greatly abraded the hill until probably the site of Laudonnère's fort has become the channel of the river. The site has been fortified several times since. During the rebellion a considerable earthwork was erected there by Florida troops, but the encroachments of the river have already swept away the site.

Laudonnère had found the Indians very friendly, and this peaceable disposition was by him assiduously cultivated. Trinkets and small presents were exchanged for the provisions which they liberally provided, and on several occasions the French lent their aid in making war on the enemies of the friendly tribes about them.

The chief or cacique of the tribe which inhabited the country between the mouth of the St. Johns River and St. Augustine was named Satourioua, or Satouriva, and in his intercourse with the French and Spanish he exhibited a remarkable sagacity and fidelity, as well as a dignity unlooked for in a savage.

Laudonnère describes his first meeting with this chief in these words: "We found the Paracoussy Satourioua under an arbor, accompanied by fourscore Indians at the least, and appareled at that time after the Indian fashion, to wit: with a great hart's skin, dressed like chamois and painted with devices of strange and divers colors, but of so lively a portraiture and representing antiquity with rules so justly compassed that there is no painter so exquisite that could find fault therewith. The natural disposition of this strange people is so perfect and so well guided that without any aid and favor of arts they are able by the help of nature only, to content the eye of artisans; yet even of those which by their industry are able to aspire unto things most absolute.

"The paracoussy now brought us to his father's lodging, one of the oldest men that lived upon the earth. Our men regarding his age began to make much of him, using this speech, Ami—ami—that is to say friend, whereat the old sire showed himself very glad. Afterwards they questioned with him concerning the course of his age; whereunto he made answer showing that he was the first living original from whence five generations were descended. M. de Ottigni having seen so strange a thing turned to the man praying him to vouchsafe to answer him to that which he demanded touching his age. Then the old man called a company of Indians, and striking twice upon his thigh, and laying his hand upon two of them, he showed him by signs that these two were his sons ; again, smiting upon their thighs, he showed him others not so old who were the children of the first two ; which he continued in the same manner until the fifth generation. But this old man had his father alive, more old than himself, and this man, which seemed to be rather a dead carcass than a live body, for his sinews, his veins, his arteries, his bones and other parts appeared so clearly that a man might easily tell them and discern them one from another, and both of them did wear their hair very long, and as white as possible, yet it was told us that they might yet live thirty or forty years more by the course of nature, although the younger of them both was not less than two hundred and fifty years old." *

Laudonnère employed the Indians to assist him in finding gold, and sent various boat expeditions to the head-waters of the St. Johns River. It is reported, though unlikely, that one of his officers penetrated the interior as far as the Mississippi.

Some of his men appear to have been dissatisfied with the position assumed by their leader. They accused him of setting up a regal state, and also of having obtained a knowledge of the location of gold which he concealed from the rest of the company. Through the influence of these disaffected ones a conspiracy was organized to depose Laudonnère. He got rid of several of the disaffected ones, however, by sending them back to France in a vessel which was returned for supplies at this period. Subsequently the discontent increased, and Laudonnère was confined for fifteen days upon one of the vessels in the river, while the mutineers set about equipping two small vessels which he had built

---

* Laudonnère's Narrative, translated by Hakluyt.

for exploration. After rifling the fort of such supplies as they needed, they set sail in these two ships on a piratical expedition. One of these vessels, having been separated by a gale from its consort, captured a Spanish ship, and after various adventures was finally captured and the crew destroyed. The other, after having exhausted its supplies, returned to the colony, and four of the leaders were tried and shot for mutiny.

Hearing that there were white captives among the Indians who resided further south, Laudonnère sent word that he would pay a considerable ransom for their delivery. Soon after there appeared two Spaniards who had been wrecked fifteen years before. They had adopted the costume of the natives—long hair, *et preteria nihil*. They reported that there had also been saved several women who had married and consented to live among the Indians.

The vessel sent to France for supplies not having returned, the garrison were threatened with an exhaustion of their stores. During all this time the French seem to have made no effort to cultivate the ground, expecting either that they would be supplied from home or that the Indians would furnish all that was required for subsistence. Their store of presents having become exhausted, however, the Indians became very niggardly and exacting, and finally declared that they were unable to supply any sort of provisions. At this Laudonnère seized a chief of one of the tribes inhabiting the territory to the south, and demanded of the Indians a large amount of provisions as a ransom. This he did not succeed in securing, and only engendered in the Indians an unfriendly spirit, which prompted them later to give to Menendez information of the location and condition of the French forces. He finally obtained supplies from some of the tribes to the north, among which was one inhabiting the sea islands, whose ruler was a beautiful queen. Finding themselves in danger of starvation, the French set about constructing a vessel to return home. They were diligently pushing on the work of construction when there appeared off the coast an English fleet under the command of Sir John Hawkins, who put into May River for water. Laudonnère entertained the English with the best he had, even killing sheep and poultry that he had been saving to stock the country. This hospitality was reciprocated by Sir John, who, seeing their desperate condition, offered to transport the whole company to France. Though he pledged his word to land them on the shores of France before touching England, Laudonnère refused his offer, fearing, as he said, "least he should attempt somewhat in Florida in the name of his mistress."

Sir John Hawkins, however, with a generous humanity, consented to sell to the French one of his vessels, and suffered them to assess its value. With the vessel the English admiral delivered to them a thousand rounds of ammunition, twenty barrels of flour, five barrels of beans, a hogshead of salt, with wax for candles, and, as he saw the Frenchmen were barefooted, fifty pairs of shoes. Having delivered these things to the French, Sir John sailed away bearing with him the blessings of these forsaken Frenchmen. Alas! their enjoyment of the fruits of the Englishman's humanity was destined to be short-lived.

CHAPTER VII.

THE UNFORTUNATE EXPEDITION UNDER RIBAULT.—FOUNDING OF ST. AUGUSTINE BY MENENDEZ, 1565. — ATTACK UPON THE FRENCH SETTLEMENT ON THE ST. JOHNS RIVER.

THE Huguenots in France had not forgotten their friends in Florida, though the dissensions at home had turned their attention away from all but the plottings and schemings about them. Desiring to succor and strengthen the colony, Coligni had secured a fleet of seven vessels, four being of considerable size. These he placed in command of Captain Ribault, who had taken out the first expedition. Ribault quickly recruited a company of six hundred and fifty persons, among whom were said to be many representatives of good families, about five hundred being soldiers.

The fleet sailed from Dieppe in May, 1565, and after a long but uneventful voyage reached Florida in safety.

By some means information had been sent to the Spanish Court that an expedition was fitting out for the succor of the Huguenot colony in Florida. It has been said that this knowledge emanated from those about the French sovereign, though it is by no means necessary that it must have come from such a source. The enemies of the Protestants were numerous and bitter all over France, and the recruiting and equipment of the expedition could have been no secret.

Philip II. determined not to allow any encroachment on the territory, which he claimed by the right of his subjects' former expeditions of discovery and by gift from the Holy See. Not only was he unwilling to see Florida occupied by foreigners, but of all persons none were more objectionable than Protestants, upon whom he looked as upon those without the pale of Christianity, who only lived as enemies of God, to disseminate a wicked creed, and war upon His holy faith. The very instrument for the execution of the plans of this bigoted monarch seems to have been at hand. Don Pedro Menendez de Avilla, had acquired wealth and distinction as a naval officer. This knight was now desirous of the honor of driving the French from Florida. Menendez was of aristocratic birth, a man of great firmness of will and tenacity of purpose; a brave commander, with a superior sagacity and knowledge of human nature, and withal a most zealous and devoted Catholic. The name of Menendez has been held up to the world as the symbol of all that is malignant, heartless, and cruel. If we are to judge of men's actions in the past by the motives that prompted them, as we are asked and expected to do in all things which happen in our own day, then by such a test the actions of Menendez must be less harshly considered. That he believed the rooting out of the Protestant colonization and their faith from the shores of the New World was God's work, there can be no doubt. His devotion to the propagation of the Catholic religion in Florida, and the sacrifices which he made to extend and continue the teachings of that faith, prove beyond a doubt his sincerity and fervent zeal. His conciliatory measures toward the savages so entirely within his power, and his efforts to instruct the tribes all over Florida, which met with such marked success, will go far to prove that his nature was not wantonly cruel. The purpose of his expedition, the object for which he had enlisted nearly three thousand persons, transporting them into an unknown continent, and, as is said, investing of his own means nearly five million dollars, was to prevent the propagation of heretical doctrines on the shores of the New World. As Menendez expressed it, it was "to prevent the Lutherans from establishing their abominable and unreasonable sect among the Indians." It should also be remembered that an edict of Ribault's had been published when he undertook his expedition, "that no Catholic at the peril of his life should go in his fleet, nor any Catholic books be taken."

Besides it is not improbable that the French prisoners, who were nearly all put to death by Menendez, were destroyed in the belief that by this course alone could his own position in his isolated location be made safe.

The little band with Laudonnère were waiting for fair winds to sail away from Florida in the ship they had purchased of the English when the fleet under Ribault arrived off the mouth of the river May, on the 29th of August, 1565. Four of the seven vessels were too large to enter the river, but the other three were brought up to the settlement, and at once began to land the supplies. Ribault now assumed the command, and all thought of departure was dismissed. This course was most acceptable to Laudonnère, who had only consented to abandon the plan of colonization from the force of his straitened circumstances and the demands of his company. He had declared that it made his heart grieve to leave "a place so pleasant that those who are melancholic would be forced to change their humor," and to possess which they had given up home, and friends, and fortune, and undergone perils of land and water.

While the fleet of Ribault was making its long voyage across the Atlantic, Menendez was pushing forward his equipment of a fleet to follow and expel the French from Florida. If he succeeded he was to have the title of marquis, a large tract of land, and the freedom of all the ports of New Spain. A salary of ten thousand dollars and the title of Adelantado was conferred upon him at the outset. He secured a fleet of thirty-four vessels, which he fully equipped, providing the means from his private fortune. But one vessel, with two hundred and fifty soldiers and their equipment, was provided by the crown. Learning the object of the expedition, volunteers flocked to his standard until he soon had a force of nearly three thousand men, including a party of twenty-six monks and priests. Impatient of delay Menendez put to sea on the 1st of July, with his flag-ship the *El Pelayo* and about two-thirds of his fleet, ordering the remainder to rendezvous at Porto Rico as soon as their equipment was completed. Scarcely had the fleet of Menendez left the port of Cadiz before a severe storm was encountered that separated the vessels, and sank and disabled so many that on his arrival at Porto Rico, on the 9th of August, he found but six ships under his command. The courage of their leader was undaunted, though a general despair pervaded the fleet. In the destruction wrought by the mighty elements he pictured the hand of God, and revived the spirits of his followers by the assurance that the Almighty had reduced their numbers that "His own arm might achieve the victory, and His glory be exalted." Learning that a Spanish vessel bearing letters to himself had been intercepted by the French fleet, he determined to sail for Florida at once, without waiting for the remainder of the fleet. On the 28th of August, the day set in the calendar of the Romish Church to the honor of St. Augustine, the fleet came in sight of the Florida coast, probably near Cape

Canaveral. Here they learned the location of the French colony, and sailing northward, on the 4th of September came in sight of the four French ships, which lay off the mouth of the river May (St. Johns). During the night a council was held on board the vessel of the Spanish admiral, in which the majority of the captains urged a delay until the remainder of the fleet could arrive from Spain. Menendez courageously refused to listen to such a plan, and gave orders for an attack at daybreak. The Frenchmen, however, displayed more of discretion than boldness, and upon the approach of the Spanish fleet, put out to sea. According to Laudonnère's account, "the Spaniards seeing that they could not reach them by reason that the French ships were better of sail than theirs, and also because they wou'd not leave the coast, turned back and went on shore in the river Seloy, which we call the river of Dolphins, eight or ten leagues from where we were. Our ships returned and reported that they had seen three Spanish ships enter the river of Dolphins, and the other three remained in the road ; further, that they had put their soldiers, their victuals, and munitions on land. . . . And we understood by King Emola, one of our neighbors, which arrived upon the handling of these matters, that the Spaniards in great numbers were gone on shore, which had taken possession of the houses of Seloy, in the most part whereof they had placed their negroes, which they had brought to labor, and also lodged themselves and had cast divers trenches about them."*

The Spanish priest Mendoza gives the following account of the foundation of St. Augustine : "On Saturday, the 8th day of September, the day of the Nativity of our Lady, the general disem-

---

* Laudonnère's Narrative, French's Historical Collections, p. 332.

barked with numerous banners displayed, trumpets and other martial music resounding, and amid salvos of artillery. Carrying a cross I proceeded at the head, chanting the hymn Te Deum Laudamus. The general marched straight up to the cross, together with all those who accompanied him ; and kneeling they all kissed the cross. A great number of Indians looked upon these ceremonies, and imitated whatever they saw done. Thereupon the general took possession of the country in the name of his Majesty. All the officers then took an oath of allegiance to him as their general, and as Adelantado of the whole country."

Near the site of the Indian village of Seloy was thus laid the foundation of the first town built by the Caucasian in America. At this time and place was also introduced that curse and blight upon the fairest portion of our country, African slavery, whose train of evils has not been confined to the Southern negroes, but has extended to the white race, and throughout the length and breadth of our common country.

Especially to Florida has this iniquitous system been the cause of unnumbered woes. For an account of the misfortunes which slavery wrought upon this State prior to the rebellion of 1861, the reader has only to consult Gidding's "Exiles of Florida." It is certain that African slavery was at this time introduced into North America, though several writers have evinced a desire to overlook this important fact of history. The evidence, however, is too plain for denial, the original agreement with Philip the Second having granted to Menendez the right to take with him five hundred negro slaves. Whether or not he took this number is not material.

In commemoration of the day on which he arrived off the coast, Menendez gave to the new town the name of St. Augustine, which it has continued to bear for more than three hundred years. The precise spot where the Spaniards landed is uncertain, though it is not unlikely that it was near the ground on which the Franciscans erected their house, now the United States barrack.

While Menendez was making haste to fortify his position at St. Augustine, Ribault was preparing to descend the coast, and by a sudden attack capture the Spanish fleet and cut off the settlement. This plan was ineffectually opposed by Laudonnère. His opposition to the plan of action adopted may have been the cause of his failure to accompany the expedition. Removing the artillery and garrison to his fleet, and leaving in the fort the non-combatants, including women, children, and invalids, to the number of two hundred and forty under the command of Laudonnère, Ribault set sail to attack the Spaniards on the 10th of September.

They bore rapidly down until in sight of the Spanish vessels anchored off the bar of St. Augustine. Before the enemy were reached, and the fleet collected for action, Ribault found himself in the midst of one of those gales which occur with suddenness and violence on the coast of Florida at different periods of every fall. The tempest rendered his ships unmanageable, and finally wrecked them all at different points on the coast south of Matanzas Inlet.

Menendez had watched the French ships as they approached St. Augustine. Observing the severity of the storm he was satisfied that the fleet could not beat back in its teeth should they escape shipwreck, and therefore their return was impossible for several days after the storm should cease. Determined to seize the favorable opportunity to attack the fort on the St. Johns, he gathered a picked force, and with eight days' provisions began a march across the country under the guidance of two Indians who were unfriendly to the French. The march proved difficult on account of the pouring rains and their ignorance of the country. The swamps and "baygalls," many of them waist-deep with water, proved so embarrassing that it took three days of laborious marching amidst great discomforts to cover the distance of fifty miles between the two posts. Immediately on the departure of the ships, Laudonnère had set to work with the force at his command to repair the breeches in the fort. These had been made when they expected to return to France. He also began to so discipline his men as to be a guard to the post. For several days the regular watches were kept up by the captains who had been appointed, but as the gale continued they began to feel confident that no attack would be made while the weather was so inclement, and therefore ceased to be vigilant. On the night of September 19th the gale had been very severe, and at daybreak, finding the captain of the watch was in his quarters, the sentinels went under shelter. At this very moment the soldiers under Menendez were in sight, kneeling in prayer. From prayers they rushed to the attack; gaining entrance into the fort without much opposition, they began an indiscriminate slaughter. Laudonnère with twenty men sprang from the walls and escaped into the woods, from whence he made his way across the marshes to a small vessel in the river, which had been left in charge of Captain Jaques Ribault, a son of the admiral. From thence they proceeded directly to France without making an effort to find their companions of Ribault's fleet or to learn their fate.

An order from Menendez to spare the women, children, and cripples, put a stop to the massacre, though it is said, "to escape death they were forced to submit to slavery." The French account says that all the men who escaped instant death were hung to the limbs of neighboring trees. This may be exaggerated, but it is certain that the Spaniards suspended the bodies of some of the Frenchmen, and set up this inscription, "No por Franceses, sino por Luteranos" (we do not do this as unto Frenchmen, but as unto Lutherans). Menendez found in the fort six trunks filled "with books well bound and gilt, from which they did not say mass, but preached their Lutheran doctrines every evening; all of which books he directed to be burned."

CHAPTER VIII.

SHIPWRECK OF RIBAULT'S FLEET.—MASSACRE BY MENENDEZ.

FEARING lest Ribault should have escaped destruction in the storm, and returning, should make an attack during his absence, Menendez hurried back to St. Augustine. He took with him only fifty men, the rest being left under the command of his son-in-law, De Valdez, who was ordered to build a church on the site selected by Menendez, and marked by the erection of crosses. After the completion of the church, De Valdez was to use every effort to strengthen the captured fort.

Arriving at St. Augustine, Menendez was hailed as conqueror, and having been escorted into the place by the priests and people who had been left behind, a solemn mass was repeated, and a Te Deum chanted to celebrate the victory.

Several of Ribault's vessels were wrecked between Mosquito and Matanzas inlets. Strange as it may appear, in the destruction of the whole fleet but one life was lost from drowning. It now often happens on the sandy portion of the Florida coast, that vessels will be driven high upon the beach by the force of the swell, and there left by the receding tide in a sound condition.

About two hundred men had collected on the southern barrier at Matanzas Inlet, while a larger party with Ribault were gathered on the same barrier, further to the south. The Indians soon after reported to Menendez a large body of men at an inlet four leagues south which they were unable to cross. He therefore marched with a body of forty men for the inlet, and arrived at Matanzas the same evening. His course was probably down the beach on Anastatia Island, as the account speaks of his ordering the boats to keep abreast of him on the march.

Having come to the mouth of the inlet one of the Frenchmen swam across, and reported that the party there assembled belonged to one of the vessels of Ribault's fleet. Menendez returned the man in a boat, and offered a pledge of safety to the French captain and four or five of his lieutenants who might choose to cross over and hold an interview. Upon this pledge the captain crossed over in the boat with four of his companions. These begged of Menendez that he would provide them with boats that they might cross that inlet and the one at St. Augustine, and return to their fort, twenty leagues to the north. Upon this Menendez informed them of the capture of the fort and the destruction of the garrison. The captain thereupon besought that they be furnished with a vessel to return to France, observing that the French and Spanish kings were loving brothers and the two nations at peace. Menendez, in reply, asked if they were Catholics; to which it was answered that they were of the New Religion. Then Menendez answered that if they had been Catholics he would feel that he was serving his king in doing them kindness, but Protestants he considered as enemies against which he should wage war unceasingly, both against them, and against all that should come into the territory of which he was adelantado, having come to these shores in the service of his king, to plant the Holy Faith, in order that the savages might be brought to a knowledge of the Holy Catholic religion.

Upon hearing this, the captain and his men desired to return and report the same to their companions, and were accordingly sent back in the boat. Soon after observing signals or signs from the opposite shore, the boat was sent over to know what was their pleasure.

The French then endeavored to make some terms for a surrender, with the privilege of ransom. There being many members of noble and wealthy families among them, as much as fifty thousand ducats was offered for a pledge of safety. Menendez would make no pledge, simply sending word that if they desired they could surrender their arms and yield themselves to his mercy, "in order that he might do unto them what should be dictated to him by the grace of God." The French seem to have had an instinctive feeling that it would fare hard with them should they yield themselves to the Spaniards; yet they were so wholly demoralized and disheartened by the misfortune that had befallen them, that after much delay and parley they finally sent word to Menendez that they were willing to yield themselves to be dealt with as he willed. The French were therefore transported across the sound in parties of ten at a time. As each boat-load was landed, Menendez directed that the prisoners be led behind "the scrub," and their hands pinioned behind their backs. This course he declared to them to be necessary, as he had but a small number of men in his command, and if left free it would be an easy matter for the French to turn upon him and revenge themselves for the destruction of their fort and Laudonnère's command. In this manner was secured the whole body of the French who had collected on the southern shore of Matanzas Inlet, to the number of two hundred and eight men. Of this number eight in response to an inquiry declared themselves to be Catholics, and were sent to St. Augustine in the boat. The remainder were ordered to march with the Spanish soldiers on their path back to the settlement. Menendez had sent on in advance an officer and a file of soldiers with orders to wait at a designated spot on the road, and as the parties of Frenchmen came up, to take them aside into the woods and put them to death. In this manner the whole party were killed, and their bodies left on the sands to feed the buzzards.

Menendez had hardly returned to St. Augustine before he learned that there was a larger body of Frenchmen assembled at the spot where he had found the first party, who were constructing a raft on which to cross the inlet. Hurrying back with his troops he sent across a boat with a message to the commander, whom he rightly conjectured was Ribault himself, that he had destroyed the fort on the St. Johns, and a body of those who were shipwrecked, and promising him a safe conduct if he wished to cross over and satisfy himself as to the truth of this report. Ribault availed himself of this offer, and was shown the dead bodies of his men who had been so cruelly murdered. He was allowed to converse with one of the prisoners who had been brought in the company of the Spaniards. This man was one of the eight who were Catholics and were spared from the former company.

Ribault endeavored to negotiate for the ransom of himself and his men, offering double the sum before named by the French captain, but Menendez refused to listen to any terms except an unconditional surrender. After ineffectually offering a ransom of 200,000 ducats, the French admiral returned to his party, and informed them of the demands of the Spaniard. In spite of the terrible fate of their comrades, which should have served as a warning of what awaited themselves, one hundred and fifty of the company, including Ribault, decided to surrender to the Spanish captain.

These were transported to the island and disposed of in the same manner as the former body of prisoners, saving only a few musicians, and four soldiers who claimed to be Catholics—in all, sixteen persons. Two hundred of the French refused to trust themselves to the Spaniards, preferring the chances of preserving their lives on the inhospitable beach until they could find a way to escape to a more friendly country. These retreated back to their wrecked ships, and began to construct a fort and a small vessel to return to France, or at least to leave the fatal shores of Florida.

Menendez soon after determined to break up their camp, fearing the presence of so large a body of his enemies in his midst. Having fitted out a fleet of three vessels to co-operate by water, Menendez marched his soldiers a journey of eight days from St. Augustine. Here he found the fugitives encamped and prepared to resist an attack. Without delay, the Spaniards were led to battle. The French, being poorly equipped, fought at a disadvantage, and were soon forced to retire beyond the reach of the cannon of the fleet. Having captured the fortification, Menendez sent word to the French that if they would surrender he would spare their lives. A portion of the French refused to trust the pledge of the Spanish captain, and withdrew to the woods. These were never heard of more. The remainder came to the Spanish camp and surrendered.

After destroying the fort and setting fire to the wrecked vessels and the ship the French had begun to build, the Spaniards sailed back to St. Augustine, bringing with them one hundred and fifty of the Frenchmen. To this remnant of the proud army of Ribault the pledges given by Menendez were faithfully kept.

It is difficult to believe that the unfortunate condition of these shipwrecked Frenchmen, far from their kindred or race, thrown destitute upon desolate shores, and begging so earnestly for life, did not move the heart of Menendez to feelings of pity. Doubtless a regard for his own safety united with a furious fanaticism to effectually seal up the springs of charity in his breast.

The earlier experiences of Menendez in his wars against the Protestants of the Netherlands, had been in a fallow field for the cultivation of humanity. In those struggles Pope Pius V. is said to have commanded Count Santafiore to take no Huguenot prisoners, but instantly to kill every one who should fall into his hands.*

Let us hope that the sands of Florida will never again be reddened by blood spilled by the hand of the bigot or partisan.

The results achieved by Menendez occasioned great rejoicing at the court of Spain. Letters of gratitude and commendation were sent to him by Philip II. and the Pontiff Pius V. The pope's letter is an able and dispassionate epistle. After lauding the virtues of Menendez, he declares to him that the key-note to his inspiration and the motive of his labors, should be to prevent the "Indian idolaters" from being scandalized by the vices and bad habits of the Europeans.

As the exaggerated reports of the cruelties practiced by Menendez spread through Europe, an intense and bitter feeling was excited. Indignation pervaded the breasts of the French nation at the destruction of their fellow-countrymen, although the king, Charles IX., failed, in fact even refused, to take notice of the slaughter of his faithful subjects. A petition from nine hundred

---

*Catena, Vita de Pio V., p. 85. "He complained of the count for not having obeyed his command to slay instantly whatever heretic fell into his hands."

widows and orphans of those who had sailed on the fatal expedition with Ribault, was unheeded by this sovereign. That the fate of the Huguenots was merited as the common enemies of Spain, France, and the Catholic religion, was the openly avowed sentiment of this unnatural and unpatriotic king.

Feeling the insecurity of his position, from which there was no place of retreat in case of a successful attack from a foreign foe or the neighboring Indians, Menendez applied himself, with the utmost diligence, to strengthening the defense of his new town. At the same time he instituted such measures as should insure a permanent settlement, and the establishment of civil rights and privileges.

I have stated that the place where Menendez landed was probably near the present United States barracks. While I have been unable to discover any authentic records bearing upon this point, the weight of Spanish testimony confirms the belief that the Spaniards first landed near the point stated. On the other hand, Romans, in his history of Florida, published in 1775, says: "After leaving St. Sebastian River, going south, we next meet the mouth of St. Nicholas Creek, on the point to the north of which the first town was built by the Spaniards, but they soon removed it, for convenience sake, to its present site."

This St. Nicholas is now called Moultrie Creek, in honor of a lieutenant-governor of the province during the British occupancy, who built at its mouth an elegant country residence, which he called Bella Vista. It is situated six miles south of St. Augustine, and empties into the Matanzas River. Besides the explicit testimony of Romans, there is a certain amount of negative testimony to discredit the statement that an Indian town was located on the present site of St. Augustine.

First, the location at the mouth of Moultrie Creek would have been a more desirable location for an Indian town than the site of St. Augustine, because the land at St. Augustine was low ground (by some writers said to have been a marsh, though others say it was an oak hummock). It must have been subject to overflow at the periods of very high tides, and always exposed to the force of gales. There is also good reason to believe that there was water or low ground between the southern end of the town and the fort, and, moreover, there are no signs of Indian occupation within the city proper. There are many traces of an Indian settlement to the north of the city, on the lands of Mr. Williams and in that vicinity, and all accounts agree that there was an Indian town there in the early Spanish times. There are acres of Mr. Williams's land that are so thickly strewn with oyster shells as to render its cultivation difficult.

However the facts may be as to the location of the first landing of Menendez and the attendant ceremonies, it is certain that, soon after, the foundations of the town were laid on its present site, and the town, with its fortifications, regularly laid out. The city was originally planned to be three squares one way by four the other. At this time a stockade or fortification was built upon or near the site of the present fort. At about the same period a parish church and hall of justice were erected and civil officers appointed.

During the winter succeeding the settlement of the Spaniards at St. Augustine, there was a great scarcity of provisions in the colony, so that the settlers were forced to forage upon the neighboring Indians, and to depend upon such supplies of fish and game as they might secure. The danger which attended any expeditions for hunting rendered this but a meager source of supply. Satouriva, the chief of the Indians, who inhabited the territory to the north, between St. Augustine and the St. Johns River, had been a friend of Laudonnère, and from the time of the destruction of the French he continued unceasingly to wage war on the Spaniards. His method of warfare exhibited the same bravery and cunning that has since become characteristic of the Indians, never being found when looked for—ever present when unexpected. By the constant harassing attacks, encouraged by this chief, the Spaniards lost many valuable lives, among them Juan Menendez, nephew of the governor.

To obtain supplies to relieve the distress of his colony, Menendez undertook a voyage to Cuba. The governor of the island was through jealousy unwilling to render him any assistance, and he would have fared badly had he not found there four of his vessels, which had been left in Spain with orders to follow him, but, meeting with many delays, had but lately arrived in Cuba.

With these vessels he returned to his colony, only to find that during his absence a portion of the troops had mutinied. The mutineers had imprisoned the master of the camp, who had been left in command, seized upon what provisions were remaining, and taking possession of a small vessel arriving with stores, had set sail for Cuba.

Menendez with consummate tact succeeded in rousing the flagging interest of his colony in the extension of the true religion, and managed by his courage and presence to remove the causes of dissension. Desiring to be rid of a portion of his colony who had proved querulous, lazy, and inimical to his interest, he sent a body of them, numbering one hundred, back to Cuba in one of the vessels going for supplies. The return of this vessel was anxiously looked for, as the colony had again begun to suffer from a scarcity of provisions and from sickness. Without waiting for affairs to become desperate, Menendez sailed for Cuba to obtain the needed supplies. Upon his arrival he found the governor of Mexico there, but so disparaging had been the reports of those who had deserted his standard, that he was advised to give up his unprofitable enterprise, and the succor he requested was refused. His courage but rose as his circumstances became more adverse, and, determined not to relinquish his undertaking nor return empty-handed to his famishing colony, he pawned his jewels and the badge of his order for a sum of five hundred ducats, with which he purchased the necessary provisions, and hastened back to Florida. Upon his return he was rejoiced to find that the distress of his colony had already been relieved. Admiral Juan de Avila had arrived from Spain with fifteen vessels and a thousand men, a large quantity of supplies, and what was most gratifying to Menendez, a letter of commendation from his sovereign.

Availing himself of the force now at his command, Menendez set out on an expedition to establish forts and missionary stations at different points along the coast, as had been his intention since his first landing in Florida. Several of these posts were at this time established by him in the territory then embraced in Florida, the most northerly station being on the Chesapeake Bay, which was the northern boundary of the possessions claimed by Spain. Priests or friars were left at each of these stations to instruct the Indians. While establishing these missionary posts for introducing Christianity among the Indians, Menendez became convinced that if the establishments were to be maintained, and the most important work of teaching the natives continued, he must have larger means and greater forces at his command. Hoping to obtain this aid from his sovereign, he set out for Spain in the spring of 1567. Upon his arrival he was welcomed by the king with many flattering attentions and assurances of aid in the furtherance of his plans for propagating the Catholic faith.

CHAPTER IX.

EXPEDITION AND RETALIATION OF DE GOURGES.

WHILE Menendez was occupied in Spain in forwarding the interests of his colony, in France plans were being formed and a secret enterprise undertaken for an attack on the Spanish posts in Florida.

Most inflammatory and exaggerated accounts of the massacre at Fort Carolin had been published throughout France.

One account says of the Spaniards that, after taking the fort, "and finding no more men, they assailed the poor women, and after having by force and violence abused the greater part, they destroyed them, and cut the throats of the little children indiscriminately, . . . they took as many of them alive as they could, and having kept them for three days without giving them anything to eat, and having made them undergo all the tortures and all the mockings that could be devised, they hung them up to some trees that were near the fort. They even flayed the king's lieutenant and sent his skin to the King of Spain, and having torn out his eyes, blackened with their blows, they fastened them on the points of their daggers, and tried who could throw them the greatest distance." *

The French king had refused to listen to the appeals of the relatives and friends of the Huguenots who had been exterminated

---

* Hakluyt's translation.

in Florida ; but, distressed by the destruction of their countrymen and the harrowing accounts of the massacre, many of the nation had long felt it a mortification that an outrage so gross should have received neither redress nor rebuke.

Among those whose jealous regard for the national honor was touched by the conduct of the French king, and in whose breast burned fiercely the fires of revenge, was the Chevalier Dominique de Gourges. Appearing as he does in history as the avenger of the sad destruction of his countrymen, in an expedition undertaken without solicitation, at his own expense, and at the risk of forfeiting his life by the command of his king, even if he should be successful, it is but natural that his character should have been extolled and his virtues exalted by all writers who have admired his chivalrous courage.

De Gourges was born of noble parentage, at Mount Marsan in Guienne, and was said to have been a Catholic, though this is denied by the Spanish historians. His life had been spent in arms in the service of his king in Scotland, Piedmont, and Italy. His career was that of an adventurer, ever ready to risk life to acquire honor and reputation, and having little desire to amass riches. While serving in Italy against the Spaniards, he was taken prisoner and consigned to labor as a galley slave. This ignominious treatment of a soldier of his birth and rank left in his mind an unappeasable hatred of the Spaniards. His period of servitude was cut short by the capture of the Spanish galley upon which he served by Turkish pirates, from whom in turn he was liberated by Romeguas, the French commander at Malta. His experience during his imprisonment and escape seems to have opened his eyes to the opportunities for plunder upon the seas. Soon after his release he entered upon a marauding expedition to the South Seas, in which he secured considerable plunder. He had but recently returned home, and retired to enjoy in quiet the property acquired in his ventures, when the news of the destruction of Ribault's colony reached France. Eager to retaliate by a severe punishment this outrage upon his countrymen, De Gourges sold his property, and with the sum realized and what he could borrow on the credit of an alleged commercial venture, purchased and equipped a fleet of three small vessels, one of which was nothing more than a launch.

Deeming it impolitic to make known the object of his voyage, he obtained a license to trade and procure slaves on the coast of Africa. He enlisted for a cruise of twelve months a force of one hundred and eighty picked men, many of whom were gentlemen adventurers. He had been careful to secure one at least of the men who had escaped with Laudonnère from Fort Carolin. M. de Montluc, the king's lieutenant in Guienne, a friend of De Gourges, rendered him valuable assistance in securing his equipment. On the 2d of August, 1567, he left Bordeaux, but was delayed by a storm eight days at the mouth of the river Garonne. Afterward, having put to sea he was driven by stress of weather far out of his course, and encountered so severe a gale as to nearly wreck the fleet on Cape Finisterre.

One vessel, in which was his lieutenant, was blown so far out of its course that for fifteen days it was supposed to be lost, which caused him all "the trouble in the world," as his people earnestly besought him to return. The missing vessel, however, met him off the coast of Africa. Land was then kept in sight until they reached Cape Verde; "thence taking the direct route to the Indies, he sailed before the wind upon the high seas, and having crossed over, the first land which he made was the island of Dominica." From thence proceeding he stopped in the island of St. Domingo to weather a gale, and at the island of Cuba for water, which he had to take by force, for he says: "The Spaniards are enraged as soon as they see a Frenchman in the Indies. For although a hundred Spains could not furnish men enough to hold the hundredth part of a land so vast and capacious, nevertheless it is the mind of the Spaniards that this New World was never created except for them, and that it belongs to no man living to step on it, or breathe in it save to themselves alone."

De Gourges had not revealed the real object of the expedition until, after leaving the island of Cuba, he assembled all his men, and declared to them his purpose of going to Florida to avenge on the Spaniards the injury which had been done to the king and to all France. He set before them the treachery and cruelty of those who had massacred Frenchmen, and the shame that it was to have left so long unpunished an action so wicked and so humiliating, and the honor and satisfaction that would redound to them in removing from the escutcheon of France this foul blot. The spirit of the address was suited to the French temper, and they professed themselves ready to fight for the honor of France wherever the captain should lead. Proceeding on the voyage the fleet passed the bar of the St. Johns River in sight of the forts which Menendez had constructed at the mouth of the river. The Spaniards, mistaking them for their own vessels, fired two guns as a salute, which was returned by the French, desiring to continue the deception. The fleet sailed north and entered the St. Mary's River, where they found a large body of Indians prepared to dispute any attempt to land. Seeing this, De Gourges made friendly demonstrations, and sent out the man who had been with Laudonnère. The Indians readily recognized the Frenchman, and were delighted to find that the strangers were of that nation, and enemies of the Spaniards. The chief proved to be Satouriva, the firm friend to Laudonnère. After learning the purpose of the expedition, Satouriva promised to join the command at the end of three days with his whole force of warriors, declaring himself eager to revenge the many injuries he had himself received as well as the wrongs inflicted on the French.

Among Satouriva's tribe was a white child, a refugee from Laudonnère's colony, who had escaped at the massacre at Fort Carolin, and been protected and reared as a son by the old chief, though the Spaniards had made strenuous efforts to secure possession of him or compass his death. This child, named Peter de Bré, whom Satouriva had so faithfully defended, he now brought to the French ships together with his warriors as he had agreed. Being joined by the Indians, De Gourges set out across the country under the guidance of the chief, Helecopile, to attack the two forts at the mouth of the river. The Indians had promised to bring the command to the fort on the north side of the river by daybreak, but, owing to the difficulty in following the intricate paths and fording deep creeks, they were nine hours marching four leagues, and the sun was rising as they reached the vicinity of the Spanish fort. This fort was built on Batton Island, near what is now Pilot-town. The other fort was nearly opposite, in the vicinity of the present village of Mayport. Both were armed with the cannon taken from the French at the capture of Fort Carolin.

The Spaniards, not fearing a land attack upon the fort on Batton Island, had neglected to clear away the woods in the vicinity, so that the French were concealed until they were close upon the fort. As they rushed from their cover the Spanish sentinel fired twice, when he was pierced by the pike of Olotoraca, an Indian chief, nephew of Satouriva. The Spanish garrison were at breakfast, and before they could be summoned the fort was filled with the French and Indians. So complete was the surprise that there was but little resistance. "As many as possible were taken alive by command of Captain Gourges, in order to do to them as they had done to the French."

As soon as the Spaniards whose lives were spared in the attack could be secured, De Gourges embarked as large a portion of his soldiers as the boats at his disposal would carry, and hurried to cross the river and attack the fort at Mayport. The Indians, now wild with excitement, threw themselves into the water and kept alongside of the boats, swimming with their bows and arrows held above their heads. The Spaniards in the fort had by this time begun to realize the situation, and directed the fire of their guns upon the boats and Indians. Their excitement and alarm were so great that they did not perceive a difference between the French and Indians, and seeing so great a multitude approaching, they broke in terror and fled from the fort before the French reached its walls. The garrison of the two forts was near a hundred and forty men, all but fifteen of whom were either killed in the attacks or slain by the Indians as they attempted to reach the mainland.

The capture of these two forts occurred on the eve of the first "Sunday after Easter, 1568." Crossing to the fort first taken, De Gourges rested on Sunday and Monday. Scaling ladders and other preparations for an attack on the main fort were in the meantime being prepared. While here, a Spanish spy disguised as an Indian was recognized by Olotoraca, and brought to De

Gourges. From him it was learned that the French force was estimated at quite two thousand men, and that the garrison of Fort Matteo (formerly Fort Carolin) was two hundred and sixty men.

Hearing this report, De Gourges was more anxious than ever to make an immediate attack. He directed the Indians to advance, some on each side of the river, and to take up a position in the vicinity of the fort. Early on the morning of the next day he moved his forces up the river, and, as he says, "gained a mountain covered with forests, at the foot of which was built the fort." He had not intended to attack the fort until the day after his arrival, but, while posting his men and the Indian forces, it happened "that the Spaniards made a sally with sixty arquebusiers * to reconnoiter his forces."

This body he succeeded in cutting off from the fort and totally destroying. Seeing the fate of so large a portion of their garrison, the remainder of the Spaniards left the fort in the hopes that they might make their way to St. Augustine. Entering the woods they were everywhere met by the Indians. None escaped, and but few were taken alive. Entering the fort, the French found a number of fine cannon beside a great quantity of arms, "such as arquebuses, corslets, shields and pikes."

The Frenchmen were now upon the scene of the massacre of their countrymen, and the taunting irony of the tablet erected by Menendez was before their eyes. The spirit of vengeance was aroused. Ordering all the Spaniards who had been taken alive to be led to the place where they had hung the Frenchmen, De Gourges rebuked them in scathing terms. He declared they

---

* The arquebuse was a rude musket exploded with a slow match.

could never undergo the punishment which they deserved, but it was necessary to make an example of them that others might learn to keep the peace which they had so wickedly violated.

"This said, they were tied up to the same trees where they had hung the Frenchmen, and in the place of the inscription which Peter Menendez had put over them containing these words in the Spanish language: 'I do this not as to Frenchmen, but as to Lutherans;' Captain Gourges caused to be graven on a pine tablet with a hot iron: 'I do this not as to Spaniards or mariners, but as to traitors, robbers, and murderers.'"

One of the Spaniards is said to have confessed that he had hung up five Frenchmen with his own hand, and acknowledged that God had brought him to the punishment he deserved. The next day while frying fish an Indian set fire to a train of powder laid by the Spaniards which had not been discovered, and the whole interior of the fort was thereby destroyed. Being aware that his forces were too weak to hold the country, and having accomplished all that he had crossed the ocean to perform, De Gourges completed the destruction of the forts, and, bidding adieu to the Indians, sailed away for France. The fleet arrived at La Rochelle on the 6th of June, after a voyage of thirty-four days. The loss of life in the enterprise had been but "a few gentlemen of good birth," a few soldiers in the attacks, and eight men on the patache or launch, which was lost at sea. Being received "with all honor, courtesy, and kind treatment," by the citizens of La Rochelle, where he remained a few days, De Gourges then sailed for Bordeaux. The Spaniards being advised of his arrival and what he had done in Florida, sent a large ship and eighteen launches to surprise and capture him. This formidable fleet arrived in the roadstead of La Rochelle the very day of his departure.

The head of De Gourges was demanded and a price set upon it by the King of Spain, but, though his acts were repudiated by the French king, he was protected and concealed by Marigny, President of the Council, and by the Receiver of Vacquieulx, until, after a time, he was the recipient of marked honors at the French court and died in 1582, "to the great grief of such as knew him."

"That De Gourges deserves censure, cannot be denied ; but there will always exist an admiration for his courage and intrepid valor, with a sympathy for the bitter provocation under which he acted, both personal and national ; a sympathy not shared with Menendez, who visited his wrath upon the religious opinions of men, while De Gourges was the unauthorized avenger of undoubted crime and inhumanity. Both acted in violation of the pure spirit of that Christianity which they alike professed to revere under the same form." *

---

* Fairbanks' History of St. Augustine, p. 107.

CHAPTER X.

RETURN OF MENENDEZ.—ATTEMPT TO CHRISTIANIZE THE INDIANS.— ATTACK UPON ST. AUGUSTINE BY SIR FRANCIS DRAKE.—MURDER OF THE FRIARS.

WHILE these events were transpiring Menendez had completed his equipment, and sailed with a fresh supply of men and means for his colonies in Florida. His first information of the disaster which had overtaken his posts on the St. Johns was received after he arrived at St. Augustine. So humiliating a disaster as the capture of three of his forts well fortified and garrisoned with four hundred trained men, was the occasion of no little mortification and vexation to this gallant knight, especially since the victors were the avengers of the former colonists, and the forces that accomplished the affair were so greatly outnumbered by his soldiers, who were also well defended by strong forts. To add to the discouragement the condition of the colony at St. Augustine was found to be most distressing. The garrison was nearly naked, the colonists half starved, and the attacks of the Indians growing more frequent and reckless as the weakness and despondency of the Spaniards became more apparent. The intrepid and indomitable spirit of Menendez did not bend under these obstacles and reverses which would have crushed a nature of ordinary mold. His extraordinary and comprehensive genius opened a way, in the midst of almost superhuman difficulties, for the maintenance of his colony and the extension of the Catholic faith, the objects to which his life was now devoted. Perceiving the insecurity of the garrisons at a distance from each other and the principal post, he wisely concluded to preserve his forces entire at St. Augustine, and thus maintain the colony and a base of operations. The spread of the Catholic faith he determined to secure by inducing the different tribes of Indians to receive and support one or more missionaries or teachers. At the earnest solicitation of Menendez large numbers of priests, friars, and brothers of the various religious orders of the Catholic Church had been sent to Florida by the King of Spain. Mission-houses were built all over the country from the Florida capes on the south to the Chesapeake on the north and the Mississippi on the west, to which these teachers, being mostly Franciscans, were sent. By the mildness of their manners, the promises of future joys and rewards which their teachings declared, and the interest excited by the introduction of the arts of civilized life, they gained a powerful ascendency over the native tribes, that promised at one period the conversion of the whole North American Indian race to the religion and customs of their Christian teachers. This would have been an achievement that would have amply compensated for all the efforts, treasure, and lives expended by the Europeans in the conquest of the New World. In fact it would have been a wonderful revolution that might well have been considered a miraculous dispensation of Providence.

It is due to the grandly comprehensive conception of Menendez that there was initiated this plan of mission stations through the Floridas, which so nearly accomplished this happy result. That the ultimate success of the efforts to Christianize the Indians was not attained was probably owing to the political changes that occurred in Europe in the eighteenth century. In both France and Spain the Jesuits fell into disgrace, and the most rigorous measures of suppression and banishment were adopted against them. The Jesuit missions in Florida shared the fate of their order in the Old World, and thus was the encouraging prospect of Christianizing the Indians swept away forever.

Under Menendez and his immediate successors whom he named and who followed his counsels were founded those missionary establishments, whose ruins have been at a late period a subject of curious investigation throughout Middle Florida. Romans ("History of Florida," New York, 1775) states that in his time there was an old bell of one of these mission houses lying in the fields near Alachua. Hon. Wilkinson Call, United States Senator from Florida, who is somewhat of an antiquarian, has informed the writer that near his birthplace in Leon County are to be found the ruins of another of these Spanish missions. The early inhabitants of the region being filled with superstition and a belief that the ruins were the remains of an establishment of the buccaneers, threw the bell into a neighboring pond, from which it has been rescued within a late period.

Menendez, finding that the interests of the colony were neglected at the Spanish Court, and that the maintenance of the colony was daily impoverishing himself, resolved to return permanently to Spain, where he hoped that his influence would be able to accomplish more benefit to the undertaking in Florida than could be expected to accrue from his presence in the territory. Leaving the province under the command of his nephew, Don Pedro Menendez, he sailed for Spain in 1572. Upon his arrival all the honors of the court were lavished upon him, and his counsels were eagerly sought in the various affairs of state.

He was not destined to enjoy his honors long, nor to reap new laurels in the European wars of the Spanish crown. In the midst of his glory his career was suddenly ended by his death from a fever, in 1574. His rank and memory are perpetuated in the Church of St. Nicholas, at Avilès, by a monument, on which is inscribed the following epitaph :

"Here lies buried the illustrious Captain Pedro Menendez de Avilès, a native of this City, Adelantado of the Province of Florida, Knight Commander of Santa Cruz, of the Order of Santiago, and Captain General of the Oceanic Seas, and of the Armada which his Royal Highness collected at Santander in the year 1574, where he died on the 17th of September, of that year, in the fifty-fifth year of his age."

Following out the instructions of Menendez, De las Alas, now governor of Florida, assembled a council from the different missions in the province for the purpose of considering methods of extending the Catholic faith. In pursuance of the advice of this council embassies were sent to all the tribes of Indians for several hundred miles around St. Augustine.

Spanish garrisons and many Spanish monks to teach the Indians had already been received into the towns east of the Appalachicola River. In 1583 the Chickasaws, Tocoposcas, Apacas, Tamaicas, Apiscas and Alabamas, received the missionaries. At this period the Catholic faith was recognized as far west as the Mississippi, and as far north as the mountains of Georgia.

The Franciscans and Dominicans had been the first to represent the monks in the New World. Afterward came the Fathers of Mercy, the Augustines, and the Jesuits.

Although Florida was included in the diocese of the Bishop

of Cuba, it was decided to establish a convent of the Order of St. Francis at St. Augustine. I find the name originally given this convent was the "Conception of Our Lady," though it is generally referred to as St. Helena.

This name St. Helena was applied to all the establishments throughout the province, of which the great Franciscan house at St. Augustine was to be the center.

Sailing in September, 1585, there arrived soon after in the West Indies a fleet of twenty-six vessels which had been fitted out by private persons in England to cruise against the Spanish commerce, and placed under the command of Sir Francis Drake, with the vice-admirals Frobisher and Knolles. After sacking St. Jago, raising a contribution of twenty-five thousand ducats on St. Domingo, and doing great injury to the Spanish shipping in the Caribbean Seas, they steered for Florida on their homeward voyage. Passing up the coast when abreast Anastatia Island, on the 8th of May, 1586, they sighted a tower or look-out station on the shore. Satisfied that it was some Spanish station the admiral ordered the boats manned and landed a body of troops on the island. Advancing toward the look-out, they perceived across the bay a fort, and further up a town built of wood.

In defiance of King Philip's order prohibiting foreigners, on pain of death, from setting foot in the province of Florida, the admiral sent General Carlisle, of the land forces, with a small body of soldiers to enter the town.

The sentinel on the island had probably retreated to the fort, as the Spaniards, without parley, opened fire upon the English boat as soon as it came within range of their guns. Perceiving that the Spaniards intended to oppose his landing, and having too small a force to make an attack upon the fort, General Carlisle withdrew to the vessels which were anchored off the bar. That evening a small boat was observed approaching the fleet from across the bay. As the boat came near, the music of a fife was heard, and the breeze bore to the ears of the English the familiar notes of the Prince of Orange's march. The fifer proved to be a French musician who had been captured, probably with Ribault's men, and who had taken advantage of the panic which the presence of the English fleet was then causing, to make his escape. He reported that the fort had been abandoned, and offered to conduct the English to the town. In the morning Sir Francis crossed the bay, and finding the fort deserted, as the Frenchman had reported, he took possession of the same and hoisted the English flag. The fort at that time was called San Juan de Pinos, and was but a rude structure built of logs and earth, and without a ditch. The palisades were built of cabbage palmettoes driven in the ground. The platforms were constructed by laying the bodies of pine trees horizontally on each other, and filling an intervening space with earth well rammed. Upon these platforms were mounted fourteen brass cannon, of what caliber is not mentioned.

The garrison numbered one hundred and fifty soldiers. Their retreat had been so precipitous that they neglected to remove the paymaster's funds, and a chest containing ten thousand dollars in silver fell into the hands of the English. It is to be hoped that this unsoldierly conduct met with exemplary correction at the hands of the *corregidors*, after the British sailed away.

"Whether the massive, iron-bound mahogany chest still (1858) preserved in the old fort is the same which fell into the hands of

Drake, is a question for antiquarians to decide; its ancient appearance might well justify the supposition."*

The next day the English marched toward the town; but it is said that they were unable to proceed by land, owing to heavy rains having lately fallen, and therefore returned to the fort and embarked in boats. Proceeding up the sound, as the boats approached the town, the Spaniards made a show of resistance; but, on the first discharge from the British marines, they fled into the country, leaving the town at the mercy of the invader. After pillaging the town and destroying the gardens, Sir Francis Drake made no further delay, but continued on his voyage to England. The Spanish account says he burned the town in revenge for the killing of his sergeant-major. The place and this attack were considered of so much importance, that after the arrival of Sir Francis in England, an engraving of "Drake's descent upon St. Augustine" was made, which "represents an octagonal fort between two streams; at the distance of half a mile, another stream; beyond that the town with a look-out and two religious houses, one of which is a church and the other probably the house of the Franciscans, who had shortly before established a house of their order there. The town contains three squares lengthwise and four in width, with gardens on the west side.

"Some doubt has been thrown on the actual site of the first settlement by this account; but I think it probably stood considerably to the south of the present public square, between the bar-

---

* Fairbanks' History of St. Augustine, p. 112. This chest has since been broken into fragments and sold to visitors as souvenirs of the old Spanish occupation. After the last chips had been disposed of, any old pieces of mahogany were substituted, until the memory of the chest had faded away, and the trade in mahogany splinters became unremunerative.

racks and the powder-house. Perhaps Maria Sanchez (Santa Maria) Creek may have then communicated with the bay near its present head, in wet weather and at high tides isolating the fort from the town. The present north ditch may have been the bed of a tide creek, and thus would correspond to the appearance presented by the sketch. It is well known that the north end of the city has been built at a much later period than the southern, and that the now vacant space below the barracks was once occupied with buildings. Buildings and fields are shown on Anastatia Island, opposite the town. The relative position of the town, with reference to the entrance of the harbor, is correctly shown on the plan, and there seems no sufficient ground to doubt the identity of the present town with the ancient locality." *

I have thought that the first town may have been built on the more western of the two peninsulas lying between Santa Maria Creek and St. Sebastian River. This would correspond with the plan published by Drake, and if we assume that the town, being built of wood, was entirely destroyed by Drake, and afterward rebuilt on its present site, the statement of Romans finds confirmation, that the first site, having been found ineligible, the location was changed to its present situation. At the time of Drake's invasion the town was said to be rapidly growing, and to have contained a church, a hall for the judges of Residencia, and other public buildings.

The Spanish governor (Don Pedro Menendez, a nephew of the founder) set himself diligently to work to rebuild the town. In the prosecution of this work, a considerable pecuniary assistance was received from Spain and Cuba, and it is

---

* Fairbanks, pp. 113, 114.

probable that the first stone buildings were erected about this period.

Much attention was at this time devoted to the temporal and spiritual welfare of the Indians. Father Rogel, who had come to Florida with the Adelantado Pedro Menendez, had learned the Indian language, and at least one of the Indians had been taken to Spain, and instructed in the Spanish language and the tenets of the Church. The Indians were considered desirable neighbors, and were encouraged to dwell near the castle, and even within the city. On a map drawn as early as 1638 the spot now occupied by the old Catholic cemetery near the head of Tolomato Street is marked "Hermitage of our Lady of Guadalupe, with the territory occupied by the Indians of the town Tolomato." Large numbers of Franciscan missionaries continued to arrive at St. Augustine, and adventurous monks, who had pined in their convents in the Old World for more work to do, found room for their energies in Florida, as the adventurous soldiers had done before them.

Early in the seventeenth century one of these Franciscans wrote a book called "La Doctrina Cristiana" in the Yemassee dialect. This volume, which is said to have been the first book written in the language of any of the North American Indians, has received an extended notice at the hands of Buckingham Smith, Esq. The labors of the missionaries were not without difficulties and discouragements, nor free from dangers. Toward the close of the sixteenth and at the beginning of the seventeenth century there were several of the worthy fathers who sacrificed their lives in noble efforts to instruct the Indians.

Padre Martinez, accompanied by two other learned and pious priests, arrived off the coast in a small vessel from Spain. Father

Martinez, being blown ashore while reconnoitering the coast in a small boat, was murdered by the Indians of Fort George Island. His companions taking alarm at the fate of their brother returned at once to Cuba.

In 1598 a most cruel and unprovoked assault was made by the Indians upon two pious fathers within sight of the castle at St. Augustine. Besides the Indian village near the gates there was another Indian town about a quarter of a mile north of the castle, situated on the creek called Cano de la Leche. The Spaniards called the place Nombre de Dios, and until after the English possession of Florida (1763-1784) there stood a stone chapel on the spot called " Nostra Senora de la Leche." This chapel was used by the English as a hospital, and fell into disuse and neglect after the Indian tribes ceased to reside peacefully in the vicinity of the town. As it was neither safe nor convenient for the inhabitants of the city to worship there, the vestments which had been given to the chapel by the King of Spain were removed. The crucifix taken from it is yet preserved in the cathedral at St. Augustine. The ground on which this chapel stood is still owned by the Catholic Church, and a new chapel was built in 1874 by Bishop Verot on the ruins of the old church ; but the severe gale of 1878 unroofed this, and at present only two of the coquina walls are standing. The location is immediately adjoining on the east the grounds of General Dent's cottage and young orange grove on the right, as you go out of the city gates by the shell road. The name of the Indian village here located was called Topiqui.

Father Pedro de Corpa had established a chapel and mission at Tolomato, and Father Blas Rodriguez another at Topiqui. Among the pupils at Tolomato was the son of the chief of

Guale, a province embraced by what is now called Amelia Island. This young chief was too full of animal spirits and the wild Indian nature to readily adopt habits required by the Franciscans. Having repeatedly offended against the proprieties of the mission, Father Corpa was compelled to publicly censure his conduct. The high spirit of the young chief rebelled at this reproof, and he at once withdrew from the mission. The good priest anticipated no evil and sought no protection. Not so the young chief. His heart was full of bitterness. Gathering a band of warriors from his own nation, he returned to St. Augustine determined on revenge. Approaching Tolomato in the dusk of evening, he burst into the chapel, and murdered Father Corpa at the altar. The Indians then cut off the worthy father's head and set it upon a pole, while his body was cast into the woods and never found. The young chief urged that an end should be made of all the missionaries in the province, saying that the friars had heaped upon the Indians injuries, and robbed them of their liberty and customs, while promising them all manner of good things, of which none were as yet received ; and thus they were compelled to labor and be deprived of all the pleasures which their ancestors enjoyed, in the hopes of receiving heaven.

The Indians of Tolomato were grieved at the death of their teacher, and urged the young chief to fly from the punishment which the Spanish governor would surely inflict. He replied that the Spaniards desired to make them all slaves, and that the penalty for the death of one priest was as severe as for the destruction of the whole body. Thus urged, they followed their leader to the village of Topiqui, where they seized Father Rodriguez, and informing him of the death of Father Corpa, declared that the same fate awaited him. In vain did the pious friar reason, in vain did he supplicate them not to commit so foolish a sin. The arguments and tears of the priest were of no avail. Finding the Indians determined to take his life, he begged the privilege of saying a last mass. "The permission was given, and there for the last time the worthy father put on his robes, which might well be termed his robes of sacrifice. The wild and savage crowd, thirsting for his blood, reclined upon the floor, and looked on in sullen silence, awaiting the conclusion of the rites. The priest alone, standing before the altar, proceeded with this most sad and solemn mass, then cast his eyes to heaven and knelt in private supplication, where the next moment he fell under the blows of his cruel foes, bespattering the altar at which he ministered with his own life's blood. His crushed remains were thrown into the fields, that they might serve for the fowls of the air or the beasts of the forests; but not one would approach them except a dog, which, rushing forward to lay hold upon the body, fell dead upon the spot, says the ancient chronicle; and an old Christian Indian, recognizing it, gave it sepulture in the forest." *

Other missions also were destroyed by this mad band of savages, but the zeal of the Franciscans was unabated, and they continued for several years to make many converts among the Indians.

In 1611 the prelate St. Francisco Marroz, "custodio from the convent of St. Francisco of the Havanna, together with the St. Helena," Fr. Miguel de Annon, and Fr. Pedro de Chocas, fell martyrs by the hands of the Indians, who are said to have pillaged the town after having driven the inhabitants to seek protection under the guns of the fort or stockade.

---

* Fairbanks, p. 119.

The now-apparent danger of a total destruction of the settlement by the Indians, who had begun to learn their own strength and the weakness of the Spaniards, opened the eyes of the governor to the necessity of more effective defense of the town. The plan of defense, embracing the castle and lines of stockades at both ends of the town with stone bastions, was initiated in the early part of the seventeenth century, though not completed for many years.

In 1640 many Apalachian Indians were brought to St. Augustine, and compelled to labor on the fort and at other works of defense. These Indians were nominally hostages for the allegiance of a very numerous tribe who lived in Middle Florida, and had made numerous ravages on the Spanish missions between 1635 and 1638. Finding peaceful measures of no avail, the Spaniards marched against them, and, after several victories, brought away a large number of captives. These were kept steadily at work until 1702, when they were released through the efforts of the Franciscan friars. This remission, however, was granted by the Spanish crown only during the peaceful conduct of their tribe, and until their services should again be required. It does not appear that the Apalachians ever again labored on the fort.

[1655-1737.]
CHAPTER XI.

PLUNDER OF THE TOWN BY CAPTAIN DAVIS.—REMOVAL OF THE YEMASSEE INDIANS.—CONSTRUCTION OF THE FORT.—BUILDING OF THE FIRST SEA-WALL.—ATTACKS OF GOVERNOR MOORE AND COLONEL PALMER.

The town of St. Augustine had continued to grow, and ninety years after its foundation was said to contain three hundred householders. This statement may be correct, as the town was afterward partly burned (1702), though Romans, more than a hundred years later, says there were not three hundred houses in his time.

The parish church at this period (1655) was said to have been built of wood, as the bishop of the diocese (Cuba and Florida) was unable to provide a better structure, his income being less than five hundred dollars per annum. In 1771 De Brahm says the churches were all built of stone. The city was allowed during the latter part of the seventeenth century a vicar, a parochial curate, and a superior sacristan, and a chaplain was attached to the fort. The convent of St. Francis was in a prosperous condition, having under its charge fifty brethren, greatly respected and very zealous for the conversion of the Indians.

In 1665 Captain Davis, an English buccaneer, sailed from the West Indies along the Florida coast for the purpose of intercepting the Spanish treasure fleet returning from Mexico. While waiting their coming he plundered St. Augustine as a diversion, no opposition being made by the inhabitants, who retired into the fort to assist the garrison of two hundred men in defending this structure. The castle was at that time an octagon flanked by two round towers.

In 1584 Captains Barlow and Armada, by the authority of Sir Walter Raleigh, had taken possession of the rivers and lands of the northern coast of Florida (South Carolina). As late as 1663 England claimed Florida as a part of the Carolinas, and in the right acquired by Henry VII. from its discovery by Cabot. In 1670 an English colony was established near Beaufort, South Carolina. The Spaniards resented this encroachment upon their territory, and in 1675 projected an attack upon the South Carolina colony, which was unsuccessful. These attacks and counter-attacks between the Spanish and English continued until the Spanish evacuation in 1763.

In 1680 Don Juan Marquez de Cabrera, having been appointed governor, entered vigorously upon the work of strengthening the defenses of the town and extending the work of the missions.

Soon after entering upon his duties the governor became annoyed at the hostile conduct, either real or fancied, of Chief Nichosatly of the Yemassees. This tribe of Indians was very powerful, and possessed many flourishing towns in Florida, lying adjacent to the English settlements on the north.

Cabrera accused him of rendering aid to the British settlers, contrary to his duties as a subject of the King of Spain.

Nichosatly denied having assisted the English, and professed loyalty to the Spaniards and the Catholic religion.

Cabrera was unwilling to trust his assurances, and condemned him to be publicly executed as a traitor. This conduct was as extraordinary as was that of the Indian ; for it is said that he exhibited a remarkable Christian temper, forgiving his enemies, and exhorting his friends not to avenge his death. This advice was not followed, unfortunately for the Spanish interests. The English used this injury to excite the Yemassees to a fierce war, and the Spaniards were soon driven from all their settlements north of the St. Johns River. Cabrera was soon after recalled in disgrace by the King of Spain, but the evil he had done was irreparable, and from this time the Spanish influence among the Indians began to decline.

Governor Cabrera had accumulated a large quantity of material, consisting of stone, oyster-shell lime, cement, timber, and iron for the prosecution of the work on the fort. His successors continued to collect supplies as fast as their means would allow. From 1693 to 1701 the governor, Laureano de Torrez-y-Ayala, kept constantly in operation two lime-kilns. He also had thirty stone-cutters employed in getting out the stone from the quarries on Anastatia Island, and eight yokes of oxen hauling the coquina to the landing on Quarry Creek.

In 1687 Don Juan de Aila volunteered to go to Spain and procure for the colony the assistance of men and supplies, of which it stood in great need. This he did, providing his own vessel, and, as a reward for his efforts, the Spanish crown granted him a permit to import merchandise free of duty, and also to carry with him twelve negro slaves. "By a mischance, he was only able to carry one negro there, with the troops and other cargo, and was received in the city with universal joy. This was the first occasion of the reception of African slaves." *

---

* Fairbanks, p. 128. This statement is evidently in error, as I have shown from Laudonnère's account that Menendez brought negro slaves; moreover, the residents of the asylum of all slaves escaping from the British colonies, and those captured by the Indians under a standing reward, would hardly rejoice over the arrival of one negro.

The Count de Galvez, Viceroy of New Spain (Mexico including Florida) seems to have felt great interest in the Spanish settlement of St. Augustine. Upon his recommendation the council of the Indies appropriated in 1691 ten thousand dollars for building a sea-wall from the castle to the city, and two years after a further sum of six thousand dollars for building a lookout.

The work upon the sea-wall had already been begun by the governor, Don Diego de Quiroga-y-Lozada, with what means the local authorities and citizens could supply.

In 1690, finding the sea was making great encroachments, and threatened to undermine the houses, having washed with great force and effect upon the light sands of the water-front, and even up to the very dwellings, the governor called a meeting of the chief citizens of the town to take the subject under consideration. It was decided by the chief men that, in order to prevent the total loss of the great sums that had already been invested in the fort and other defenses of the town, and to protect the place from gradual destruction, and being unfitted for habitation, it was necessary to build a wall from the glacis of the fort to the public square on the north of the city, which should be a defense against the force of the sea. Two thousand dollars were contributed, of which the soldiers are said to have donated seventeen hundred, although their wages were six years in arrears.

The wall, which was begun at this time, was a slight structure, and extended only to the present basin in front of the plaza. To one who has seen the water, in severe north-easters, dashing over the present sea-wall, it seems strange that the Spaniards had not built a more extensive and efficacious protection against the sea for their metropolitan town in North America. One of the old citizens informs me that the tide rose so high during a severe storm in the fall of 1811, that boats passed freely over the streets, and the inhabitants were all obliged to withdraw from the lower story of the houses.

In 1693, Governor Don Laureano de Torrez received another thousand dollars contributed out of their wages by the soldiers, and also further assistance from the home government, with which he continued the building of the sea-wall, and the work on the fort. It is probably about this time that the Mexican convicts were employed in the construction of the castle. At one time there was said to have been one hundred and forty of these convicts in service at St. Augustine.

For several years the Spaniards had greatly harassed the English settlers in the Carolinas, having made incursions in 1675, and again in 1681, and, as a fixed policy, incited the Indians to make inroads to ravage the unprotected settlements, and carry off plunder, especially negroes. Many demands were made on the Spanish authorities for the negroes thus carried away, and also those who escaped ; but the Spaniards invariably refused to surrender the slaves, alleging that the King of Spain felt it his duty to keep the negroes under the influence of the Catholic religion.

In 1702 Governor Moore of South Carolina determined to retaliate upon the Spaniards for their conduct toward the English, by the capture of the town of St. Augustine. He induced the legislature to vote him aid to the extent of two thousand pounds sterling, and to authorize the enlistment of six hundred volunteers, and an equal number of Creek and Yemassee Indians. Impressing a number of merchant ships into service as transports, the troops were taken to Port Royal as a rendezvous, where Governor Moore joined them in September of the same year. Colonel Daniel, who is described as the life of the expedition, was made second in command, and ordered to proceed through the inland passages of the St. Johns River, and thence to attack St. Augustine by land, while the governor should enter the harbor and attack the city from his ships. The Spaniards, having notice of the advance, retired into the castle with their valuables, and a store of provisions to maintain them for four months. Colonel Daniel arrived behind the town before Governor Moore's fleet came to the harbor, and meeting with no resistance, entered at once and secured a considerable plunder which the inhabitants had been unable to remove. The next day Governor Moore arrived and entered upon a regular siege, so that the Spaniards were obliged to lie quietly within the walls of the castle. Moore, finding that his cannon were too light to effect a breach in the walls of the fort, sent a vessel to Jamaica for guns of a larger caliber. This vessel not returning, he sent Colonel Daniel in a second on the same errand. While his lieutenant was thus absent there appeared in sight two Spanish vessels, one of twenty-two and the other of sixteen guns. At sight of these Moore was stricken with such a panic that he abandoned his ships and fled across the country to Charleston. He is said, however, to have first burned the town (in part only, it is most likely), and to have previously sent to Jamaica the church plate and other costly church ornaments and utensils. This is quite likely, as the English troops occupied the parish church immediately on their entrance into the town.

Colonel Daniel secured the munitions for which he was sent, and promptly returned to St. Augustine, rejoicing in the thought that the place was now in their power. Entering the harbor he first learned of Moore's retreat upon being chased by the Spanish ships, from which he narrowly escaped.

This expedition cost the English colony six thousand pounds, for which they received only disgrace, having accomplished nothing but the imprisonment of the Spaniards for a period of three months. At the termination of the siege, the inhabitants at once applied themselves to repairing and rebuilding their houses, and the governor, Don Joseph de Zuñiga, received liberal aid from Spain in rebuilding and strengthening the town.

In 1706 the French and Spaniards under Mons. La Febour entered the harbor of St. Augustine on their way to attack Charleston. Taking a part of the garrison of the fort they proceeded on their voyage, but were obliged to retreat without accomplishing anything.

In 1717 the Spanish governor, Don Juan de Ayola y Escobar, procured a general combination of the Yemassee, Creek, Apalache, Congaree, Catauba, and Cherokee Indians, against the English settlements in Carolina.

A year after Don Antonio de Benavuedi y Malina, having been appointed governor, put a stop to the Indian hostilities against the English.

He seems to have entertained a very unfavorable opinion of the Indians, which he exhibited in an unreasonable decree against the Yemassees, exiling this tribe to a distance six leagues south of St. Augustine. The Yemassees remonstrated with the new governor against this order; stating to him that although at one time they had joined the English, after the execution of their Chief Nichosatly, yet they had since repented of that fault, and fought against them in behalf of the Spaniards; that it would be a grievous act to drive them from their fields of corn, and their houses, while the English were their enemies; that they revered the Catholic king and the holy Church, and desired to have its rites administered to them, and wished to live in peace.

The governor was obdurate, and ordered Captain Ortagas to execute his order with the troops. Thus this powerful nation, abandoning their fields almost ripe for harvest, and many cattle and hogs, were compelled to make new homes in the wilderness. It is said that many women, children, and infirm persons were left on Amelia Island; that the English killed four hundred when they found that the Indians were abandoning the country; and that of the three thousand who had resided between St. Augustine and the St. Mary's River, at the end of a year from their removal, not one-third had survived the vengeance of their enemies and hunger and disease. The removal of this tribe of Indians was impolitic on the part of the Spaniards, as the English soon after took possession of their lands, which lay between the English and Spanish settlements.

In 1725 the disputes between the English and Spaniards culminated in hostilities. The Spaniards charged the English with intruding on their lands, and the English retorted that the Spaniards had enticed away their negroes and incited the Indians against their settlements. The Spanish governor recalled the Yemassees, and having armed and equipped a body of warriors under their chief Mocano, sent them into Georgia, where they committed a general massacre.

Colonel Palmer of that colony raised a body of three hundred militia, and entered Florida, burning and destroying every Spanish and Indian settlement to the very gates of St. Augustine. The Spanish inhabitants of the country and town fled into the fort for safety; but, with execrable meanness, excluded the poor Indians, who were nearly all killed or made prisoners. The

Spaniards saved only what could be protected by the guns of the fort, which was then quite a formidable work.

The chapel of Nostra Senora de la Leche, the location of which has been described, was plundered by some of the soldiers. They stripped it of the gold and silver vessels, and taking the infant image from the arms of the figure of the Virgin Mary, brought it to Colonel Palmer, who was encamped two miles north of the city gates. This piece of sacrilege, however, was displeasing to the commander, who told the soldiers that the Spaniards would one day be revenged upon them. Having accomplished all he could hope from his small force, Colonel Palmer retired with a great booty of cattle and other plunder.

In 1737 Governor Don Manuel de Monteano, soon after taking command of the province, made the following report to the Governor-general of Cuba: "The fort of this place is its only defense; it has no casemates for the shelter of the men, nor the necessary elevation of the counter-scarp, nor covert ways, nor ravelins to the curtains, nor other exterior works, that could give time for a long defense; but it is thus naked outside, as it is without soul within, for there are no cannon that could be fired twenty-four hours." The representations of the governor received prompt attention at the Spanish Court, where it had now become recognized that the Spanish possessions in America were endangered, and unless St. Augustine was maintained, they would be irrecoverably lost.

Large appropriations of money were sent, and a garrison of seven hundred regular troops, and a number of new cannon assigned to the castle. With the means thus provided, the governor applied himself with great energy and skill in putting the fort in an excellent state of defense. The superintendence of the work was assigned to Don Antonio de Arredondo, an officer who ranked well among engineers. Bomb-proofs were constructed, a covered way made, the ramparts heightened and casemated, and redoubts extended across either end of the town, in which there were ten salient angles.*

Romans states that two of these salient angles or bastions, built of stone, stood in the southern line of redoubts, but were broken down by the English, and the material used for the foundation of the new barracks. From the statements of old residents, I am satisfied that one or more stood near the present saw-mills, and commanded the approach by the old road across the marshes of the St. Sebastian.

It is probable that the credit is due Don Arredondo for the symmetry and beauty of outline in the general design of the fort, and also for the perfection of the lines, curves, and angles in the masonry. The noble conception and perfection of detail throughout the work demonstrates the engineer to have been a man of excellent abilities, and proficient in the higher mathematics, " one of the sublimest realms of human thought."

Some of the curves in the masonry within the casemates are beautiful pieces of design. The compound circular and elliptic arch, or three-centered circular arch, which supports the incline leading from the terre-plein to the court, is said to have presented a problem too difficult for the United States engineer in charge of the repairs after the change of flags. It will be seen that the north side of the arch having fallen has been patched with a rectilinear wall, and the symmetry of the elegant lines destroyed.

---

* See Souvenir Album of St. Augustine for a view of the old lighthouse, which exhibits a salient angle protecting the gate of the inclosing wall.

CHAPTER XII.

OGLETHORPE'S ATTACK.—BOMBARDMENT OF THE FORT AND TOWN.—CAPTURE OF THE HIGHLANDERS AT FORT MOSA.—OLD FORT AT MATANZAS.—MONTEANO'S INVASION OF GEORGIA.

IN 1740 Governor Oglethorpe of Georgia, being encouraged by King George II., determined to capture St. Augustine, and thus drive the Spaniards from Florida. At his request the Carolina colonies sent him a body of four hundred troops under Colonel Vanderdussen. He also equipped a body of Creek Indians, and in May had rendezvoused at the mouth of the St. Johns River a force of two thousand men. With a portion of this force he attacked a small fort called Diego, situated on what is now known as Diego Plains (called by the inhabitants Dago), twenty-five miles north of St. Augustine, then the estate of Don Diego de Spinosa. The remains of this fort and several cannon were to be seen until a late date.

Having taken the fort after a slight resistance, he left the same in charge of Lieutenant Dunbar, and returned to the St. Johns River to await the arrival of more troops, and to allow Commodore Price, R. N., to blockade the harbor of St. Augustine with his fleet, consisting of four vessels of twenty guns each.

From the prisoners captured at Diego it was learned that the Spaniards had lately received a reinforcement of six half galleys, armed with several long brass nine-pounders, and two sloops loaded with provisions, besides which all the cattle in the neighborhood had been driven into town. The prisoners, he says, "agree that there are fifty pieces of cannon in the castle, several of which are of brass, from twelve to forty-eight pounds, It has four bastions. The walls are of stone and casemated. The internal square is sixty yards. The ditch is forty feet wide and twelve feet deep, six of which are sometimes filled with water. The counter-scarp is faced with stone. They have lately made a covered way by embanking four thousand posts. The town is fortified with an intrenchment, salient angles, and redoubts, which inclose about half a mile in length and a quarter of a mile in width. The inhabitants and garrison, men, women, and children amount to above two thousand five hundred. For the garrison the king pays eight companies, sent from Spain two years since, fifty-three men each; three companies of foot and one of artillery of the old garrison, and one troop of horse, one hundred each."

This estimate would make the garrison about nine hundred and twenty-four men, which was probably within the whole number of fighting men, as another account says there were in the town at the time, the seven hundred regulars assigned from Spain two companies of horse, and four companies of negroes, besides Indians. These negroes were probably free men, as it is elsewhere stated that they had their own officers, and though armed, by the governor, provided themselves.

Oglethorpe having been joined by more troops marched across the country, ordering the forces at Diego to advance as far as Fort Mosa, two miles north of St. Augustine, while he made an attack on the fort at Picolata. This fort was called St. Francis de Poppa, and commanded the approaches from West Florida and Mexico, and the ferry across the St. Johns River. Its remains existed until a short time since, and even yet the ditch can be traced upon the grounds of Mr. Michael Usina. If the testimony of the old residents can be relied upon, Forbes and Vignoles in their histories have fallen into error as to the location of this old Spanish fortification, describing it as on the west side of the river, while the old citizens call the fort at Picolata "Fort Poppa."

Forbes says Picolata's ancient fort was built by the "Spaniards with square towers thirty feet high and a deep ditch about it, which is now partly filled up. The stone was brought from Anastatia Island. On the opposite side is Fort Poppa, with shallow intrenchments twenty yards square and as many from the river. A small distance back is another turret of the same size, and some groves of orange trees and oaks."

Vignoles' description (1823) is as follows: "Of the old blockhouse of Picolata nothing remains except two of the shattered walls, through which loop-holes and *meutrières* are pierced. It stands on a low bluff, and is half concealed by the luxuriant branches of surrounding trees. It reminds the visitor who views it from the river of the deserted castellated residence of some ancient feudal lord. Opposite is Fort Poppa, of which scarce a vestige remains."

William Bartram, in his "Travels through Florida," published in Philadelphia, 1791, gives an interesting description of this fort which I will also quote, as I find all knowledge of these old relics is fast being effaced from memory and accessible records. Describing his sail up the St. Johns River, he says: "At noon I came abreast of Fort Picolata, where, being desirous of gaining yet further intelligence [about it], I landed, but to my disappointment found the fort dismantled. This fortress is very ancient and was built by the Spaniards. It is a square tower, thirty feet high, pierced with loop-holes and surrounded with a deep ditch. The upper story is open on each side, with battlements supporting a cupola or roof. These battlements were formerly mounted with eight four-pounders, two on each side.

"The work was constructed with hewn stone, cemented with lime. The stone was cut out of the quarriës on St. Anastatia Island, opposite St. Augustine." Williams calls the fort on the west side of the river Fort "San Fernando."

Oglethorpe captured the Fort at Picolata without difficulty, and after considerable delay advanced his whole force upon St. Augustine. The fleet, which had by this time arrived, was moored across the harbor, and one vessel stationed off the mouth of Matanzas River, to prevent the arrival of supplies from that quarter. A company of eighty Scotch settlers from Georgia, all dressed in Highland costume, together with forty Indians, were stationed at Fort Mosa, under Colonel Palmer, with orders to avoid a battle, but to be vigilant in scouring the country, to intercept all supplies, and to encamp every night at a different place. Colonel Vanderdussen, who had marched from the St. Johns River by the beach, was ordered to build a battery at Point Quartell (north beach), while Oglethorpe, with a regiment of Georgians and the main body of the Indians, landed on Anastatia Island, and began the construction of a battery at the north end of the main island. Aware that his force was too small to carry an assault on the castle, to which the inhabitants and forces had all retired, Oglethorpe determined to reduce the fort by bombardment, while he cut off all supplies by a blockade. The site of the first battery constructed on the island has long since become the channel of the river. The high ridge to the west of the lighthouse, on which Mr. Aspinwall has lately built a small building, probably extended at least half a mile north of the present shore line. It was on this ridge that Oglethorpe built his first battery, and having mounted in it several eighteen-pound cannon, he sent a message to the Spanish governor summoning him to surrender.

The governor, Don Manuel de Monteano, a very brave and efficient officer, replied that he would be pleased to shake hands with General Oglethorpe in the fort. The general, being indignant at such a reply, opened fire upon the place, which was kept up with spirit, and many shells were thrown into the town, causing the citizens to seek shelter within the walls of the castle. The Spaniards replied with the cannon in the fort, and also diverted the attention of the British with the maneuvers of the six galleys with their batteries of nine-pounders. Captain Warren, a brave officer from the fleet, offered to lead an attack on these galleys in the night; but it was decided that the plan was too dangerous, as the galleys lay at night under the guns of the fort, where the water was too shoal to bring up any large vessels to cover the attacking party. Finding the distance too great for his fire to injure the fort, Oglethorpe began the construction of a second battery on the marsh of the island, nearer the town. This battery was called Battery Poza, and mounted four eighteen-pound cannon. The remains of this battery are still to be seen. It is located on an island in the marsh, and reached from the bay by ascending a small creek, navigable for boats at half tide. Oglethorpe is said to have buried an eighteen-pound cannon in this battery when the siege was raised, which may yet be beneath the sand of the redoubts.

While engaged in the construction of Battery Poza, the fire of the British was somewhat relaxed. Observing this, Governor Monteano sent out a detachment of three hundred men and a party of Yemassee Indians, to attack Colonel Palmer at Fort Mosa. It is said the sally was made on the night of the king's birthday, and that the British were found drinking and carousing. The former statement is incorrect, though the latter may be true. Colonel Palmer was a brave and able officer, but he seems to have had Scotch obstinacy, united with undisciplined men, to render his authority nugatory.

The camp was surprised and the Highlanders quickly overcome after Colonel Palmer was slain and the soldiers who were vigilant had been killed or made their escape. There was a tradition that Colonel Palmer was killed by Wakona, the Yemassee chief, on the spot where the soldiers had brought him the infant image fifteen years before.

This loss was a severe blow to the expedition, not so much from the loss of the men, but its effect was to depress the spirits of the command and to greatly discourage the Indians, who soon after found an excuse to withdraw. A Cherokee having killed a Spaniard, cut off his head and brought it to Oglethorpe, who spurned the Indian and called him a barbarous dog. This rebuff was made a pretext by the Indians for their desertion, and, without making known their intentions, soon after they were gone.

Meantime the bombardment continued; but it was found that, even from the nearest battery, the shot produced little effect upon the walls of the castle. The siege, which was commenced on the 13th of June, had now continued into July, with only disastrous results. The soldiers began to wilt under the extreme heat, and complain of the annoyance of the sandflies and mosquitoes. To add to the difficulty sickness appeared, and the men, never under very good control, began to desert in squads, and return across the country to their homes. The commodore, finding his provisions becoming short, and fearing the autumn gales, was unwilling to remain longer on the station. The ship at Matanzas had already withdrawn. The inlet being unguarded, the Spaniards soon succeeded in bringing in a large supply of provisions, of which they now stood in great need. Learning that the Spaniards had received succor, the troops lost all hope, and the siege was soon after raised.

It would seem, from the accounts of this blockade and the fact that supplies were brought in at Matanzas Inlet, that the old fort at Matanzas was not then standing. If this is the case, it must have been constructed immediately after Oglethorpe's departure, as the Spaniards had had a garrison in it before the English occupation, as will be seen from the following extract from Romans: "Twenty miles south [of St. Augustine] is the look-out or fort of Matanca, on a marshy island commanding the entrance of Matanca, which lays opposite to it. This fort is to be seen at a distance of about five leagues. It is of very little strength, nor need it be otherwise, as there is scarce eight feet of water on this bar at the best of times. The Spaniards kept a lieutenant in command here; the English a sergeant. Between two or three miles from this inlet or bar is another of still less note, called El Penon. Matanca Bar is known from the sea by the fort, which shows white in a clear day, when the inlet bears west, three leagues off."

I have been unable to find out at what date this fort was constructed. The natural features have greatly changed since the time of Romans even. The island has been very much washed away by the current, and will soon cease to exist at all. The bar, which must have been nearly opposite the island, has gradually worked south until now it is nearly half a mile below the fort, and a high sand ridge, a part of Anastatia Island, is between the fort and the ocean, so that, instead of being visible three leagues at sea, the fort, probably, would not be seen from the ocean at all.* Soundings on Matanzas Bar are now given as one fathom. Fort Mosa, where Colonel Palmer was killed, was built by the negro refugees from the British colonies, and was often called the Negro Fort. It was a square earthwork with four bastions, containing a well and a house with a look-out, and surrounded with a ditch. The walls of a stone house are still standing near the location of this fort, at a place called by the town's people "Moses," north of Mr. Hildreth's grounds.

Oglethorpe was greatly blamed at the time for his failure to take St. Augustine, but it is evident that the town was well protected. The north side of the peninsula, on which the town is built, was defended by the fort, about which, for a space of fifteen hundred yards, a clear space was maintained by the Spanish governors, and also by the ditch and redoubt with salient angles running from the fort to the St. Sebastian River; upon the east side of the town the galleys and the guns of the fort could prevent a landing, as the water upon the bar was too shoal to admit the passage of the English ships; upon the south was a line of redoubts again with cannon, and a water front for the approach of the galleys, while upon the west was the long stretch of boggy marshes extending for a quarter of a mile to the St. Sebastian River. No place could be better situated for defense. Had the blockade been efficient and long-continued the town must have surrendered as there was a large population to feed besides the garrison, and the very advantages of the place for defense rendered it difficult to bring in supplies.

---

* For an excellent view of this old fort, see Souvenir Album of Views in St. Augustine.

Governor Monteano was constantly sending messages to Cuba, by the way of West Florida and the Keys, for succor of provisions, and was said to have received supplies from a vessel which arrived at Mosquito Inlet, while the harbor of Matanzas was yet blockaded.

The siege was abandoned on the 10th of July. During the bombardment one hundred and fifty-three shells fell in the town, but occasioned no loss of life, and did very little damage. That the fire from the batteries was very ineffectual is evident from an inspection of the shot-holes in the walls of the old fort made by the guns of Oglethorpe's batteries which are still visible. I have counted eight indentations on the eastern face of the main fort, and two on the south-east bastion. Their penetration was barely sufficient to bury the solid shot, while the shell do not appear to have done any injury, thus exhibiting an ineffectiveness of the artillery which seems remarkable, as there were said to have been thirty mortars large and small, and ten eighteen-pound cannon in the different batteries erected by Oglethorpe, of which the farthest was not more than three-quarters of a mile distant.

This attack of Oglethorpe seems to have demonstrated to the Spanish crown the likelihood of an English occupation of their possessions in Florida. The following year large reinforcements were sent to Governor Monteano, with instructions to improve the defenses of the town in every possible way.

Finding the British colonists did not renew their attack on the town as he had anticipated, Monteano advised an invasion of Georgia and South Carolina. Accordingly an army of two thousand men was raised in Cuba, which, being dispatched to St. Augustine, was placed under the command of Governor Monteano. To this force the governor added one thousand men from the garrison of the town, including a regiment of negroes, whose officers are said to have dressed, ranked, and associated with the Spanish officers without reserve.*

With this force Monteano entered upon the invasion of Georgia; but, being opposed by Oglethorpe with great energy and skill, was entirely unsuccessful, and the expedition retired to St. Augustine. From thence the forces returned to Cuba, where the governor was imprisoned and tried for misconduct, though acquitted of the charges.

In the next year Oglethorpe endeavored to retaliate upon the Spaniards, and get possession of St. Augustine by a sudden attack which should take the town by surprise. He is said to have approached with such celerity and secresy that he arrived within sight of the town without exciting an alarm. Here he captured a small body of troops acting as a guard to the king's workmen. This capture defeated the success of his surprise, for, the absence of the guard being noticed, a body of horsemen were sent out to learn the cause of their detention, and the forces of Oglethorpe were discovered in time to close the city gates and prepare the garrison. Oglethorpe was unwilling to risk an assault on the town, and retired into Georgia, after spending two months in attempting to provoke the Spaniards to a fight without the walls of the town. During this time his troops completely devastated the surrounding country.

Up to about this period there had existed an Indian village near the site of Fort Mosa (or Moosa) called Macarizi. It was probably located on a creek now called "Baya's Creek," about two miles north of the city, though the Franciscan Father Ayeta,

---

* Williams' Florida, p. 185.

in his "La Verdad Defendida," p. 215, says that Macarizi and Nombre de Dios (Topiqui) were the same.

Soon after Oglethorpe retired Governor Monteano furnished arms and ammunition to one Pedro Christano, a Spanish Indian chief among the Yemassees, and incited incursions against the British colonists in Georgia. These were continued under the encouragement of the Spaniards until the settlements south of St. Simonds Island were entirely broken up. These hostilities, which had continued since 1725, were mutually suspended under the treaty which was concluded between England and Spain in 1748, but marauding expeditions were again entered upon in 1755. The Spanish ambassador at London, having obtained from the court of St. James an order commanding the English settlers to retire from the territory of Florida, the new governor, Don Alonzo Fernandez de Herreda, sent a company of dragoons to hasten the obedience of the English colonists. Upon a summons the English agreed to retire, but they never did so, and the next year, 1763, the provinces of the Floridas were ceded to Great Britain in exchange for Havana and the western portion of Cuba, which had been captured from the Spanish. This treaty was concluded on the 3d of November, 1762, and ratified February 10th, 1763.

CHAPTER XIII.

THE TOWN WHEN DELIVERED TO THE ENGLISH.—FORT SAN JUAN DE PINOS.—ST. AUGUSTINE AS DESCRIBED BY THE ENGLISH WRITERS 1765 TO 1775.

BEFORE the cession of the province, the fort had been completed, and presented, at the time it was delivered to the English, very much the same appearance as now. Many of the casemates had platforms about seven feet from the floor for sleeping apartments. The moat was about four feet deeper than at present, and the water battery was built in such a manner that the guns were mounted upon it instead of behind it, as at present. The high banks of sand on the north, west, and south sides of the fort have been placed there in recent times as a protection from the shot of modern guns, which would soon make a breach through almost any thickness of coquina wall. The fortress occupies about four acres of ground, and mounts one hundred guns, requiring a garrison of a thousand soldiers, though a much larger number have, on several occasions, been its garrison. Its site was well chosen for the protection of the town in the days when it was built, as its guns command the whole harbor and inlet from the sea, as also the whole peninsula to the south, upon which the town is built, the land approach from the north, and the marshes west of the town. Various dates have been assigned as the period at which the work on this fort was commenced, but of this date there is no record in this country, if there is in Spain. At the time of Drake's attack, 1586, there was an octagonal fort on or about the site of the present structure, which was built of logs and earth. In 1638, or thereabouts, the Apalachians were set to work on the fortifications of the town, and, as Menendez had applied himself to strengthening the defenses of the town after the attack of De Gourges, 1567, it is probable that this fort had been commenced before the beginning of the seventeenth century. That the Spaniards had then begun to use coquina as a building stone is to be inferred from a statement of Romans, that, in his time, one of the old houses of the town bore the date 1571. The name of the wooden fort was San Juan de Pinos, and the present fort bore the name St. John for many years. It is supposed that the old wooden structure stood near the north-west bastion, which was probably called St. John, while the south-east was named for St. Peter, the south-west was called St. Augustine, and the north-east St. Paul.

It is uncertain when the name St. Mark's was first applied to the castle, though probably during the English occupation, 1663–1684. The fort, doubtless, acquired the name from that applied to the present north river, which was called by the Spaniards St. Mark's River, at the mouth of which the fort is located. It is probably the oldest fortification now standing in the United States, and certainly the oldest which is yet in a good state of preservation. From the date at which the Apalachians began work, until the year in which the fortification was declared finished and the commemorative tablet erected, the period during which it was being built is one hundred and eighteen years. It has now been a century and a quarter since this magnificent old structure, representing the grandest military architecture of the middle ages, was completed, and two centuries and a half since its inception.

What a strange and eventful history is connected with its stone walls, its deep ditch, its frowning battlements, its dismal dungeon, and damp casemates, in the midst of which, on the north side, is its chapel with raised altar, built into the masonry, and holy water niches in the walls of the casemates.

Those who have read this history thus far will have noted the laying of its foundations by the hands of those zealous and bigoted Catholics who had exterminated a settlement of the subjects of a friendly nation, lest they should spread among the barbarous Indians heretical doctrines; the accretion of its rising walls under the hands of the unfortunate Indians, who had been loath to accept the Christian teachers and doctrine that had been forced upon them by these expungers of heresy, until, with the aid of convicts and king's workmen, the work was completed, to stand the defense of the Spanish possessions in Florida, the protection of fugitive slaves, depredating Indians, Spanish pensioners and adventurers, and the prison of many wretched Indians and whites who had fallen under the displeasure of a Spanish autocrat. For almost two hundred years the Spanish ensign had been uninterruptedly displayed from the site of this fort, when, by the treaty of 1762, it was yielded to the British, and the cross of St. George displayed from its battlements.

The year after his arrival in Florida, Governor Hereda sculptured, in alto-relievo, the Spanish coat of arms over the entrance of the fort. The tablet upon which the design is impressed is made of cement, and let into the walls of the fort. The inscription on the tablet beneath the coat of arms is as follows:

"REYNANDO EN ESPANA EL SEN^N DON FERNANDO SEXTO Y SIENDO GOV^R Y CAP^N DE ES^A C^D SA^N

AUG^N DE LA FLORIDA Y SUS PROV^A EL MARISCAL DE CAMPO D^N ALONZO FERN^{DO} HERADA ASI CONCLUIO ESTE CASTILLO EL AN OD 1756 DRI$_A^G$ENDO LAS OBRAS EL CAP. INGN^{RO} DN PEDRO DE BROZAS Y GARAY."

TRANSLATION:

"*Don Ferdinand the VI, being King of Spain, and the Field Marshal Don Alonzo Fernando Hereda being Governor and Captain General of this place, St. Augustine of Florida, and its province, this Fort was finished in the year* 1756. *The works were directed by the Captain Engineer, Don Pedro de Brazas Y Garay.*" *

An alto-relievo coat of arms, upon a cement tablet, was also placed upon the lunette, but vandal relic hunters have disfigured this tablet most aggravatingly. In the top of this tablet there is an oval-shaped hollow, which looks as if it might have been worn by the handle of a spear, or small staff of a standard. It is possible that the sentry has stood upon this wall, resting his lance on the top of this tablet for years, until this hollow has been worn three inches or more in depth, and so perfectly smooth as to have a polish over the surface of the depression.

Every part of this old work should be protected and preserved by the United States, whose property it is. With proper care, and moderate repairs from time to time, this old structure will yet remain for ages a grand old relic of medieval architecture, and a monument of the first settlement of this country by our

---

* For an excellent view of the tablet over the entrance to the fort, on which is sculptured the Spanish coat of arms and the above inscription, see Souvenir Album of Views in St. Augustine.

European ancestors. The sum of thirty millions of dollars is said to have been expended by the Spaniards in the construction of this fortification; a sum so vast that, when the amount was read to King Ferdinand VI., he is reported to have turned to his secretary, and exclaimed, "What! Is the fort built of solid dollars?"

"Of its legends connected with the dark chambers and prison vaults, the chains, the instruments of torture, the skeletons walled in, its closed and hidden recesses, of Coacouchee's escape, and many another tale, there is much to say; but it is better said within the grim walls, where the eye and the imagination can go together in weaving a web of mystery and awe over its sad associations, to the music of the grating bolt, the echoing tread, and the clanking chain." *

I have heard from native residents that tales of skeletons, etc., were never heard until after the late war; which assertion the above quotation from Fairbanks' History, published in 1858, will disprove.†

The appearance and condition of the town at the time of the English possession has been described by several writers, whose quaintness of style adds to the inherent interest of the subject.

The English surveyor-general, De Brahm, describes the place as follows:

"At the time the Spaniards left the town, all the gardens were well stocked with fruit trees, viz.: figs, guavas, plantain, pomegranates, lemons, limes, citrons, shadock, bergamot, China and Seville oranges, the latter full of fruit throughout the whole winter season. The town is three quarters of a mile in length, but

---

* Fairbanks' History and Antiquities, p. 157.

† For several views of the old fort, see Souvenir Album of Views in St. Augustine.

not a quarter wide; had four churches ornamentally built with stone in the Spanish taste, of which one within and one without the town exist. One is pulled down; that is the German church, but the steeple is preserved as an ornament to the town; and the other, viz., the convent-church and convent in town, is taken in the body of the barracks. All the houses are built of masonry; their entrances are shaded by piazzas, supported by Tuscan pillars or pilasters against the south sun. The houses have to the east windows projecting sixteen or eighteen inches into the street, very wide and proportionally high. On the west side, their windows are commonly very small, and no opening of any kind on the north, on which side they have double walls six or eight feet asunder, forming a kind of gallery which answers for cellars and pantries. Before most of the entrances were arbors of vines, producing plenty and very good grapes. No house has any chimney or fireplace; the Spaniards made use of stone urns, filled them with coals left in their kitchens in the afternoon, and set them at sunset in their bedrooms to defend themselves against those winter seasons which required such care. The governor's residence has on both sides piazzas, viz., a double one on the south, and a single one to the north; also a Belvidere and a grand portico decorated with Doric pillars and entablatures. On the north end of the town is a casemated fort, with four bastions, a ravelin, counterscarp, and a glacis built with quarried shell-stones, and constructed according to the rudiments of Marechal de Vauban. This fort commands the road of the bay, the town, its environs, and both Tolomato Stream and Matanzas Creek. The soil in the gardens and environs of the town is chiefly sandy and marshy. The Spaniards seem to have had a notion of manuring their land with shells one foot deep."

In 1770, according to De Brahm, the inhabitants of St. Augustine and vicinity numbered 288 householders exclusive of women and children, of whom 31 were storekeepers and traders; 3 haberdashers, 15 innkeepers, 45 artificers and mechanics, 110 planters, 4 hunters, 6 cow-keepers, 11 overseers, 12 draftsmen in the employ of the government, besides mathematicians; 58 had left the province, and 28 had died, of whom 4 were killed acting as constables, and two hanged for piracy.*

Another account says that at the time of the evacuation by the Spaniards, the town contained a garrison of 2,500 men, and a population of 3,200, who were of all colors, whites, negroes, mulattoes, Indians, etc. This estimate probably included the surrounding country as well as the town, as Romans a few years later made the number residing within the city much smaller. He says: "The town has, by all writers, till Dr. Stork's time, been said to lay at the foot of a hill; so far from the truth is this, that it is almost surrounded by water, and the remains of the line drawn from the harbor to St. Sebastian Creek, a fourth of a mile north of the fort, in which line stands a fortified gate called the Barrier Gate, is the only rising ground near it; this line had a ditch, and its fortification was pretty regular; about a mile and a half beyond this are the remains of another fortified line, which had a kind of look-out or advanced guard of stoccadoes at its western extremity on St. Sebastian Creek, and Fort Mossa at its eastern end; besides these the town has been fortified with a

---

* History of the Three Provinces, by Wm. Gerard de Brahm, His Majesty's Survr. Gen. for the Southern District of North America, from 1751 to 1771. A manuscript work purchased in London, in 1848, for Harvard College library, for £12 10s. The portion relating to Florida comprises 173 pages with 14 maps.

slight but regular line of circumvallation and a ditch. The town is half a mile in length, and its southern line had two bastions of stone, one of which (if not both) are broken down, and the materials used for the building of the foundation of the barracks; the ditch and parapet are planted with a species of agave, which by its points is well fitted to keep out cattle.* Dr. Stork has raised this into a fortification against the savages, and magnified it into a chevaux de frize. The town is very ill built, the streets being all, except one, crooked and narrow. The date on one of the houses I remember to be 1571 ; these are of stone, mostly flat-roofed, heavy, and look badly. Till the arrival of the English, neither glass windows nor chimneys were known here, the lower windows had all a projecting frame of wooden rails before them. The governor's house is a heavy, unsightly pile, but well contrived for the climate ; at its north-west side it has a kind of tower; this serves for a look-out. There were three suburbs in the time of the Spaniards, but all destroyed before my acquaintance with the place, except the church of the Indian town to the north, now converted into an hospital. Dr. Stork says the steeple of this church is of good workmanship, though built by the Indians, neither of which assertions is true. The steeple of the German chapel to the west of the town likewise remains.†

"The parish church in the town is a wretched building, and now almost a heap of ruins ; the parade before the governor's

---

* Spanish bayonet (Yucca Gloriosa). It bears a pyramid of white flowers, and, as also the prickly pear, by its appearance suggests the rural scenery of the tropics.

† I have been unable to find any record of the time or manner in which any German colony settled in St. Augustine.

house is nearly in the middle of the town, and has a very fine effect; there are two rows of orange trees planted by order of Governor Grant, which make a fine walk on each side of it; the sandy streets are hardened by lime and oyster shells. Dr. Stork says there were nine hundred houses at the time of the Spanish evacuation, and 3,200 inhabitants. In my time there were not three hundred houses, and at most a thousand inhabitants; these, a few excepted, I found to be a kind of outcast and scum of the earth; to keep them such their ill form of government does not a little contribute. A letter dated May 27th, 1774, says this town is now truly become a heap of ruins—a fit receptacle for the wretches of inhabitants." *

This sweeping condemnation of the whole population of the town would seem to be exceedingly unjust and unbecoming a historian.

Major Ogilvie of the British army received the town from the Spaniards, and immediately entered upon an administration of the affairs of the province which was most unreasonable and impolitic. "Major Ogilvie, in taking possession of the eastern province, by his impolitic behavior caused all the Spaniards to remove to Havana, which was a deadly wound to the province, never to be cured again."

So oppressive was the course of this commander, that it was said that not more than five of the Spanish inhabitants consented to remain in the province, and only by the efforts of the officer in command were the Spaniards prevented from destroying every house and building in the town. The governor did destroy his garden, which had been stocked with rare ornamental plants, trees, and flowers.

---

* Romans's History of Florida, New York, 1775.

By the articles of peace the King of Great Britain guaranteed "the liberty of the Catholic religion," but the prejudices of the Spaniards were deeply rooted, and the transfer of the territory was distasteful beyond measure. Governor James Grant was sent out from England to take charge of the province, and immediately, upon relieving Major Ogilvie, issued a proclamation dated October 7th, 1763, intended to conciliate and retain those Spaniards who had not withdrawn, and recall those who had, as well as to encourage persons in England to remove to Florida.

Governor Grant had been high in command at the capture of Havana. His administration of a country hitherto the seat of war between the aborigines, the original settlers, and their British neighbors, was not without many difficulties; but his management of affairs was generally very satisfactory, and showed much policy and executive ability. It was said of him that, hearing of any coolness between those about him, they were brought together at his table (always well provided) and reconciled before they were allowed to leave it. His conduct was not exempt from unfriendly criticism, however, and it was charged that he would not allow the transfer of Spanish landed interest to be good, although mentioned in the treaty; "that he reigned supreme without control, even in peace, notwithstanding the frequent murmurs of the people and the presentments of the grand juries, occasioned by his not calling an assembly, which they thought was a duty incumbent upon him. There was also a complaint of the contingent money, of five thousand pounds per annum for seven years, not being so very visibly expended on highways, bridges, ferries, and such other necessary things as the people would have wished." *

---

* Romans's History of Florida.

The Spaniards attempted to illegally transfer, and, in fact, did sell the whole of their property in St. Augustine to a few British subjects for a nominal sum. It was probably this class of conveyances that Governor Grant refused to recognize. The complaint as to the building of roads, etc., must have been without foundation, as under Governor Grant were constructed all those public roads, since known as the King's Roads, running from New Smyrna to St. Augustine, and thence to Jacksonville and the St. Mary's River. These roads were all turnpiked upon the line of surveyed routes, and are to-day the best roads in the State.

Under Governor Grant the British built at St. Augustine very extensive barracks, which were soon afterward burned. Romans thus criticises the policy of the governor in expending so large sums on military works: "The bar of this harbor is a perpetual obstruction to St. Augustine becoming a place of any great trade, and alone is security enough against enemies; so that I see but little occasion for so much fortification as the Spaniards had here, especially as a little look-out called Mossa, at a small distance north of the town, proved sufficient to repel General Oglethorpe with the most formidable armament ever intended against St. Augustine. However, there was much more propriety in the Spaniards having a fort in the modern taste of military architecture—of a regular quadrilateral form, with four bastions, a wide ditch, a covered way, a glacis, a ravelin to defend the gate, places of arms and bomb-proofs, with a casemating all round, etc., etc., for a defense against savages—than there was in raising such a stupendous pile of buildings as the new barracks by the English, which are large enough to contain five regiments, when it is a matter of grave doubt whether it will ever be a necessity to keep one whole regiment here. To mend this matter, the great barrack was built with materials brought to St. Augustine from New York, far inferior in value to those found on the spot, yet the freight alone amounted to more than their value when landed, so that people can hardly help thinking that the contrivers of all this, having a sum of money to throw away, found it necessary to fill some parasite's pockets. This fort and barrack, however, add not a little to the beauty of the prospect," as one approaches the town from the water.

When the old light-house was built I have been unable to discover. Under Governor Grant it was raised by a timber construction, and had a cannon planted on it, which was fired as soon as the flag was hoisted to notify the inhabitants and pilots that a vessel was approaching. It had two flagstaffs, one to the north and one to the south, on either of which the flag was hoisted as the vessel was approaching from the north or south.

It is possible that the old light-house was constructed in 1693, with the proceeds of the six thousand dollars appropriated by the Council of the Indies, for "building a tower as a look-out." The Spaniards kept a detachment of troops stationed there, and the tower and adjoining chapel were inclosed with a high and thick stone wall, pierced with loop-holes, and having a salient angle to protect the gate. Romans describes it, in his time, as follows: "About half a mile from the north end of the island [Anastatia] is a heavy stone building serving for a look-out. A small detachment of troops is kept here, and by signals from hence the inhabitants are given to understand what kind of, and how many vessels are approaching the harbor, either from the north or from the south. In the year 1770, fifty feet of timber framework were added to its former height, as was likewise a mast or flagstaff forty-seven feet long ; but this last, proving too weighty, endangered the building, and was soon taken down."* This old structure was repaired and a house for the light-keeper built in 1823, by Elias Wallen, a contractor, who was also employed upon the repairs made to the old "Governor's House."

The coquina ledge upon which it was built has of late years been rapidly washing away by the action of the tides, and dashing of the waves, which during the annual north-east storms are sometimes of considerable force. A storm washed away the foundations of the tower, and it fell with a crash on Sunday, the 20th of June, 1880. Thus has gone forever one of St. Augustine's most interesting old landmarks.†

The English built a bridge across the St. Sebastian River upon the old road leading over the marshes, which approached the town near the saw-mills. From some defect in construction, this bridge did not remain long. They then established a ferry, and appointed a ferry-keeper with a salary of fifty pounds sterling per annum. The inhabitants paid nothing for crossing except after dark.

---

* Romans's History of Florida.

† A very good view of this old structure is published in the Souvenir Album of Views in St. Augustine.

CHAPTER XIV.

THE SETTLEMENT OF NEW SMYRNA BY THE ANCESTORS OF A MAJORITY OF THE PRESENT POPULATION OF ST. AUGUSTINE.—THE HARDSHIPS ENDURED BY THESE MINORCAN AND GREEK COLONISTS.—THEIR REMOVAL TO ST. AUGUSTINE UNDER THE PROTECTION OF THE ENGLISH GOVERNOR.

THE proclamation of Governor Grant, and the accounts which had gone abroad of the advantages of the province, and the liberal policy adopted by the British in the treatment of colonists, induced some wealthy planters from the Carolinas to remove to Florida, and several noblemen of England also solicited grants of land in the province. Among the noblemen who secured grants of land in Florida were Lords Hawke, Egmont, Grenville, and Hillsborough, Sir William Duncan, and Dennys Rolle, the father of Lord Rolle. Sir William Duncan was a partner with Dr. Turnbull in importing a large number of Europeans for the cultivation of their lands south of St. Augustine, on the Halifax River. The persons whom these two gentlemen then induced to come to Florida are the ancestors of a large majority of the resident population of St. Augustine at the present day. In the early accounts of the place I am satisfied that gross injustice was done to these people in a reckless condemnation of the whole community. I have myself heard their descendants unreasonably censured, and their characters severely criticised. These unfavorable opinions were doubtless generated by the unfortunate position in which these immigrants found themselves. Friendless in a strange land, speaking a different language from the remainder of the inhabitants, and of a different religious belief, it was but natural that they should mingle but little with the English residents, especially after they had experienced such unjust treatment at the hands of one of the most influential of the principal men of the colony. The reader will understand the position of these Minorcans and Greeks, and the feelings they must have entertained toward the great men of the colony, after reading Romans's account of the hardships they were forced to undergo, and the difficulty they had in breaking their onerous contract. Romans says: "The situation of the town, or settlement, made by Dr. Turnbull is called New Smyrna from the place of the doctor's lady's nativity. About fifteen hundred people, men, women, and children, were deluded away from their native country, where they lived at home in the plentiful corn-fields and vineyards of Greece and Italy, to this place, where, instead of plenty, they found want in the last degree; instead of promised fields, a dreary wilderness; instead of a grateful, fertile soil, a barren, arid sand, and in addition to their misery were obliged to indent themselves, their wives and children for many years to a man who had the most sanguine expectations of transplanting bashawship from the Levant. The better to effect his purpose, he granted them a pitiful portion of land for ten years upon the plan of the feudal system. This being improved, and just rendered fit for cultivation, at the end of that term it again reverts to the original grantor, and the grantee may, if he chooses, begin a new state of vassalage for ten years more. Many were denied even such grants as these, and were obliged to work at tasks in the field.

Their provisions were, at the best of times, only a quart of maize per day, and two ounces of pork per week. This might have sufficed with the help of fish, which abounded in this lagoon; but they were denied the liberty of fishing, and, lest they should not labor enough, inhuman taskmasters were set over them, and instead of allowing each family to do with their homely fare as they pleased, they were forced to join altogether in one mess, and at the beat of a vile drum to come to one common copper, from whence their hominy was ladled out to them; even this coarse and scanty meal was, through careless management, rendered still more coarse, and, through the knavery of a providetor and the pilfering of a hungry cook, still more scanty. Masters of vessels were forewarned from giving any of them a piece of bread or meat. Imagine to yourself an African—one of a class of men whose hearts are generally callous against the softer feelings— melted with the wants of these wretches, giving them a piece of venison, of which he caught what he pleased, and for this charitable act disgraced, and, in course of time, used so severely that the unusual servitude soon released him to a happier state. Again, behold a man obliged to whip his own wife for pilfering bread to relieve his helpless family; then think of a time when the small allowance was reduced to half, and see some brave, generous seamen charitably sharing their own allowance with some of these wretches, the merciful tars suffering abuse for their generosity, and the miserable objects of their ill-timed pity undergoing bodily punishment for satisfying the cravings of a long-disappointed appetite, and you may form some judgment of the manner in which New Smyrna was settled. Before I leave this subject I will relate the insurrection to which those unhappy people at New Smyrna were obliged to have recourse, and which the great ones styled rebellion. In the year 1769, at a time when the unparalleled severities of their taskmasters, particularly one Cutter (who had been made a justice of the peace, with no other view than to enable him to execute his barbarities on a larger extent and with greater appearance of authority) had drove these wretches to despair, they resolved to escape to the Havannah. To execute this they broke into the provision stores and seized on some craft lying in the harbor, but were prevented from taking others by the care of the masters. Destitute of any man fit for the important post of leader, their proceedings were all confused, and an Italian of very bad principles, but of so much note that he had formerly been admitted to the overseer's table, assumed a kind of command; they thought themselves secure where they were, and this occasioned a delay till a detachment of the Ninth Regiment had time to arrive, to whom they submitted, except one boatful, which escaped to the Florida Keys and were taken up by a Providence man. Many were the victims destined to punishment; as I was one of the grand jury which sat fifteen days on this business, I had an opportunity of canvassing it well; but the accusations were of so small account that we found only five bills: one of these was against a man for maiming the above said Cutter, whom it seems they had pitched upon as the principal object of their resentment, *and curtailed his ear and two of his fingers;* another for shooting a cow, which, being a capital crime in England, the law making it such was here extended to this province; the others were against the leader and two more for the burglary committed on the provision store. The distress of the sufferers touched us so that we almost unanimously wished for some happy circumstances that might justify our rejecting all the bills, except that against the chief who was a villain. One man was brought before us three or four times, and, at last, was joined in one accusation with the person who maimed Cutter ; yet, no evidence of weight appearing against him, I had an opportunity to remark, by the appearance of some faces in court, that he had been marked, and that the grand jury disappointed the expectations of more than one great man. Governor Grant pardoned two, and a third was obliged to be the executioner of the remaining two. On this occasion I saw one of the most moving scenes I ever experienced ; long and obstinate was the struggle of this man's mind, who repeatedly called out that he chose to die rather than be the executioner of his friends in distress ; this not a little perplexed Mr. Woolridge, the sheriff, till at length the entreaties of the victims themselves put an end to the conflict in his breast, by encouraging him to act. Now we beheld a man thus compelled to mount the ladder, take leave of his friends in the most moving manner, kissing them the moment before he committed them to an ignominious death. Cutter some time after died a lingering death, having experienced besides his wounds the terrors of a coward in power overtaken by vengeance." *

The original agreement made with the immigrants before leaving the Mediterranean was much more favorable to them than Romans describes it. At the end of three years each head of a family was to have fifty acres of land and twenty-five for each child of his family. This contract was not adhered to on the part of the proprietors, and it was not until, by the authority of the courts, they had secured their freedom from the exactions imposed upon them that any disposition was shown to deed them lands in severalty. After the suppression of this attempt to es-

---

* Romans's History of Florida, N. Y., 1775.

cape, these people continued to cultivate the lands as before, and large crops of indigo were produced by their labor. Meantime the hardships and injustice practiced against them continued, until, in 1776, nine years from their landing in Florida, their number had been reduced by sickness, exposure, and cruel treatment from fourteen hundred to six hundred.

At that time it happened that some gentlemen visiting New Smyrna from St. Augustine were heard to remark that if these people knew their rights they never would submit to such treatment, and that the governor ought to protect them. This remark was noted by an intelligent boy who told it to his mother, upon whom it made such an impression that she could not cease to think and plan how, in some way, their condition might be represented to the governor. Finally, she decided to call a council of the leading men among her people. They assembled soon after in the night, and devised a plan of reaching the governor. Three of the most resolute and competent of their number were selected to make the attempt to reach St. Augustine and lay before the governor a report of their condition. In order to account for their absence they asked to be given a long task, or an extra amount of work to be done in a specified time, and if they should complete the work in advance, the intervening time should be their own to go down the coast and catch turtle. This was granted them as a special favor. Having finished their task by the assistance of their friends so as to have several days at their disposal, the three brave men set out along the beach for St. Augustine. The names of these men, most worthy of remembrance, were Pellicier, Llambias, and Genopley. Starting at night they reached and swam Matanzas Inlet the next morning, and arrived at St. Augustine by sundown of the same day. After inquiry they decided to make a statement of their case to Mr. Young, the attorney-general of the province. No better man could have been selected to represent the cause of the oppressed. They made known to him their condition, the terms of their original contract, and the manner in which they had been treated. Mr. Young promised to present their case to the governor, and assured them if their statements could be proved, the governor would at once release them from the indentures by which Turnbull claimed to control them. He advised them to return to Smyrna and bring to St. Augustine all who wished to leave New Smyrna, and the service of Turnbull. "The envoys returned with the glad tidings that their chains were broken and that protection awaited them. Turnbull was absent, but they feared the overseers, whose cruelty they dreaded. They met in secret and chose for their leader Mr. Pellicier, who was head carpenter. The women and children with the old men were placed in the center, and the stoutest men armed with wooden spears were placed in front and rear. In this order they set off, like the children of Israel, from a place that had proved an Egypt to them. So secretly had they conducted the transaction, that they proceeded some miles before the overseer discovered that the place was deserted. He rode after the fugitives and overtook them before they reached St. Augustine, and used every exertion to persuade them to return, but in vain. On the third day they reached St. Augustine, where provisions were served out to them by order of the governor. Their case was tried before the judges, where they were honestly defended by their friend the attorney-general. Turnbull could show no cause for detaining them, and their freedom was fully established. Lands were offered them at New Smyrna, but they suspected some trick was on foot to get them into Turnbull's hands, and besides they detested the place where they had suffered so much. Lands were therefore assigned them in the north part of the city, where they have built houses and cultivated their gardens to this day. Some by industry have acquired large estates: they at this time form a respectable part of the population of the city." *

It will be seen by the date of their removal to St. Augustine that the unfavorable comments of Romans and the Englishman whose letter he quotes upon the population of the town at the cession to Great Britain, could not have referred to the immigrants who came over under contract with Turnbull. It will also be seen that Williams speaks in very complimentary terms of these people and their descendants. I am pleased to quote from an earlier account a very favorable, and, as I believe, a very just tribute to the worth of these Minorcan and Greek settlers and their children. Forbes, in his sketches, says: "They settled in St. Augustine, where their descendants form a numerous, industrious, and virtuous body of people, distinct alike from the indolent character of the Spaniards and the rapacious habits of some of the strangers who have visited the city since the exchange of flags. In their duties as small farmers, hunters, fishermen, and other laborious but useful occupations, they contribute more to the real stability of society than any other class of people: generally temperate in their mode of life and strict in their moral integrity, they do not yield the palm to the denizens of the land of steady habits. Crime is almost unknown among them; speaking their native tongue, they move about distinguished by a primitive simplicity and purity as remarkable as their speech." †

---

* Williams' Florida, page 190, A.D. 1837.
† Forbes' Sketches, etc., N. Y., 1821.

Many of the older citizens now living remember the palmetto houses which used to stand in the northern part of the town, built by the people who came up from Smyrna. By their frugality and industry the descendants of those who settled at Smyrna have replaced these palmetto huts with comfortable cottages, and many among them have acquired considerable wealth, and taken rank among the most respected and successful citizens of the town.

[1771.]
CHAPTER XV.

ADMINISTRATION OF LIEUT.-GOVERNOR MOULTRIE.—DEMAND OF THE PEOPLE FOR THE RIGHTS OF ENGLISHMEN.—GOVERNOR TONYN BURNING THE EFFIGIES OF ADAMS AND HANCOCK.—COLONIAL INSURGENTS CONFINED IN THE FORT.—ASSEMBLING OF THE FIRST LEGISLATURE.—COMMERCE OF ST. AUGUSTINE UNDER THE ENGLISH.—RECESSION OF THE PROVINCE TO SPAIN.

GOVERNOR GRANT's administration lasted until 1771, when he returned to England suffering in health. Upon his departure the province was under the authority of Hon. John Moultrie, the lieut.-governor, for a period of three years. The spirit of liberty, which was making itself felt throughout the British provinces at the North at this time, was here in Florida exciting in the breasts of those born under the British flag a determination to demand the rights granted by the Magna Charta. Urged by leading men in the council, the grand jury made presentments setting forth the rights of the inhabitants of the province to a representative government. These presentments the lieut.-governor disregarded, but finally yielded so far as to consent to the formation of a legislature which should be elected and meet every three years. The freeholders were inflexible in their determination to have annual sessions of their representatives, and continued without representation rather than to yield. The chief justice, William Drayton, a gentleman of talents and great professional knowledge, being unwilling to yield to the pretensions of the lieut.-governor, was suspended from his office, and the Rev. John Forbes, an assistant judge, was appointed to the vacancy by Lieut.-Governor Moultrie. It was charged against Mr. Forbes that his sympathies were with the Americans of the northern colonies. The confirmation of his appointment was therefore rejected and a chief justice sent from England.

In March, 1774, a new governor arrived from England. This gentleman was Colonel Patrick Tonyn, a *protégé* of Lord Marchmont, and very zealous for the royal cause. He at once issued a proclamation inviting the inhabitants of the provinces to the North, who were attached to the crown, to remove with their property to Florida. This invitation was accepted by a considerable number of royalists. In 1776 Governor Tonyn issued another proclamation inviting the inhabitants of the towns on the St. Johns, and of the Musquitoes, to assemble and co-operate with the king's troops in resisting the "perfidious insinuations" of the neighboring colonists, and to prevent any more men from joining their "traitorous neighbors." This was met by a counter proclamation by President Batton Gwinnet, of Georgia, who encouraged the belief that the God of "armies had appeared so remarkably in favor of liberty, that the period could not be far distant when the enemies of America would be clothed with everlasting shame and dishonor." Governor Tonyn issued commissions to privateers, and held a council of the Indians to secure their alliance against the patriots of the neighboring colonies.

Upon the receipt of news of the Declaration of Independence of the American colonies, the royalists showed their zeal for the king by burning the effigies of John Hancock and Samuel Adams on the plaza, near where the constitutional monument now stands. In 1775 some privateers from Carolina captured the brig *Betsy* off the bar, and unloaded her in sight of the garrison, giving to the captain a bill signed "Clement Lamprière," and drawn on Miles Brewton, at Charleston, for one thousand pounds sterling. The cargo consisted of one hundred and eleven barrels of powder sent from London, and the capture was a great mortification to the new governor.

During the early years of the struggle between the American colonies and the mother country, St. Augustine was the British point of rendezvous and an asylum for the royalists. From Georgia and Carolina there were said to have been seven thousand royalists and slaves who moved to Florida during these years. So hazardous to the colonial interests had the British possession of St. Augustine become, that Governor Houston, of Georgia, urged upon General Howe to attack the place in the spring of 1778. This expedition was never undertaken, though Colonel Fuser, of the Sixtieth Regiment, issued a proclamation on June 27th, 1778, commanding all those who had not entered the militia to join him, as "the rebels might be expected every instant."

The inhabitants of the province, while willing to fight for the king, still demanded the establishment of a representative government. Governor Tonyn, in a letter to Lord George St. German, Secretary of State, says: "I perceive the cry for a provincial legislature to remedy local inconveniences is as loud as ever, and suggestions are thrown out that, without it, people's property is not secure, and that they must live in a country where they can enjoy to their utmost extent the advantages of the British Constitution and laws formed with their consent. But mention the expediency, propriety, reasonableness, justice, and gratitude of imposing taxes for the expenses of the government, they are all silent, or so exceedingly poor as not to be able to pay the least farthing."

In 1780 Governor Tonyn repaired both lines of defense about the town, strengthened the fortifications, and added several new works. The inhabitants complained bitterly that the burdens of the public defense fell upon them, as their negroes were kept for several months employed upon the king's works. The governor seems to have considered that loyalty to the king was not to be expected from his new subjects in Florida, or at least was to be found only among Protestants. Writing of the militia, he says: "There are several Minorcans, and I have my doubts as to their loyalty, being of Spanish and French extraction, and of the Roman Catholic religion."

About this time the British, having captured Charleston, seized a number of the most influential men of South Carolina, in violation of their parole, and sent them to St. Augustine, where they remained until exchanged in 1781. All of the number, except General Gadsden, accepted a second parole, after arriving at St. Augustine. Gadsden, refusing to receive pledges at the hands of those who had already broken them, was confined for nearly a year in the fort. These prisoners were often threatened with the fate due to defeated rebels, and perhaps were taken to view the gallows at the north-east corner of the court-yard in the fort, said to have been erected by the British.*

The pressure upon the governor, urging him to permit the enjoyment of the rights of representation granted by the king's

---

* See Souvenir Album of Views in St. Augustine.

charter, had now become so forcible that, in 1781, a General Assembly was called, consisting of an Upper and a Lower House. The former was probably composed of the crown officers, and the latter of those elected by the freeholders.

March 17th, 1781, the first Assembly met. Though Florida had been settled more than two hundred years, never before had the citizens been allowed to assemble and enact a law. The governor, in his address upon the assembling of the two Houses, was inclined to be sarcastic. He announced that the "king and Parliament," with astonishing "and unprecedented condescension," relinquished their right of taxation, provided the Legislature made due provision for defraying the expenses of the government, and this when the whole sum raised by taxation did not amount to the salary of the king's treasurer. The principal source of revenue was said to be from licenses to sell liquors.

In 1781 an event occurred most damaging to the material advancement of the province. This was an order from Sir Guy Carleton, H. B. M., Commander-in-chief in America, to General Leslie, in Carolina, to evacuate the province of East Florida with all his troops and such loyalists as wished. The inhabitants at once sent the most urgent protests against this harsh and unreasonable order, appealing to the governor and the king, by whom it was soon after revoked.

It was at the hands of an expedition fitted out at St. Augustine that Great Britain obtained possession of the Bahama Islands, which she still holds. In 1783, Colonel Devereux, with two twelve-gun vessels, and a small force of men, made a sudden attack and captured the town of Nassau, with the Spanish garrison and governor.

During the latter part of the British possession the exports of rum, sugar, molasses, indigo, and lumber had become considerable. As early as 1770 the records of the Custom-House showed the entry of fifty schooners and sloops from the northern provinces and the West Indies, beside several square-rigged vessels from London and Liverpool. In 1771 the imports were: 54 pipes of Madeira wine, 170 puncheons of rum, 1,660 barrels of flour, 1,000 barrels of beef and pork, 339 firkins of butter, and 11,000 pounds of loaf sugar. These cargoes were brought in twenty-nine vessels, of which five were from London. There were also imported about 1,000 negroes, of whom 119 were from Africa.

The average annual expenses of East Florida, while under the British flag, were £122,660 sterling, without including the pay of the army or navy. In 1778, a period of the greatest prosperity reached under the British flag, the whole value of the exports was only £48,000 sterling, or a little more than one-third of the expenses of the province.

Through the exertions of the Anglo-Saxon settlers, who had brought to the province their advanced ideas of government, agriculture, and commerce, Florida was just entering upon a career of prosperity, when it was again ceded to Spain. These constant changes, necessitating the transfer of property to the subjects of the ruling sovereign, would, of themselves, have prevented any considerable improvement in the material wealth of the province; but the treaty between Great Britain and Spain so far neglected to provide for the interests of the British subjects who had settled in Florida, that the only stipulation relating to them was one allowing them the privilege of removing within eighteen months from the time of the ratification. Whatever real property was not sold to Spanish subjects, at the end of this period, was to become the property of the Spanish Crown. Under the British there had settled in the town of St. Augustine a large number of half-pay officers of the British Government, who, with others possessing certain incomes, had greatly improved the place. It is said that those conversant with the place in 1784, spoke highly of the beauty of the gardens, the neatness of the houses, and the air of cheerfulness and comfort that seemed during the preceding period to have been thrown over the town. Florida was literally deserted by its British subjects upon the change of flags. Vignoles says: "Perhaps no such other general emigration of the inhabitants of a country, amicably transferred to another government, ever occurred." Among the British subjects, who remained and transferred their allegiance to Spain, were several families whose descendants are still living in Florida.

CHAPTER XVI.

RETURN OF THE SPANIARDS.—COMPLETION OF THE CATHEDRAL.—THE OLDEST CHURCH BELL IN AMERICA.—THE GOVERNOR'S DESIRE TO PEOPLE THE PROVINCE WITH IRISH CATHOLICS.—SOME OFFICIAL ORDERS EXHIBITING THE CUSTOMS OF THE SPANIARDS.—UNJUSTIFIABLE INTERFERENCE OF THE UNITED STATES, DURING THE "PATRIOT WAR."—FLORIDA AN UNPROFITABLE POSSESSION.—ERECTION OF THE MONUMENT TO THE SPANISH CONSTITUTION.

IN June, 1784, Governor Zespedes took possession of St. Augustine, in the name of "his most Catholic Majesty." The British Government had provided a fleet of transports to convey its subjects, and from the St. Johns River and the St. Mary's they sailed for the American colonies and the British dominions.

With the Spanish flag returned to St. Augustine the numerous company of salaried officials and crown-pensioners holding sinecure offices, and contributing nothing to the improvement of the place, and nothing to its existence but their presence. This large portion of the inhabitants, dependent upon the crown, did not always receive punctual payment of their salaries; but, with their daily allowance of rations in kind, they were enabled to exist. They generally occupied the houses belonging to the crown, which were numerous, and the rent required was but nominal. In 1764, a large number of lots in the town had been sold in confidence to Jesse Fish, a British subject, to prevent their being forfeited to the crown at the expiration of the period allowed by the treaty between Great Britain and Spain for the disposal of private property. This sale was not recognized as valid by the Spanish authorities upon their return, and one hundred and eighty-five lots were thus forfeited to the King of Spain. These lots were soon after sold at auction, on terms very favorable to the purchasers.

Upon the return of the Spaniards they at once devoted their energies to completing their house of worship. At the change of flags (1763) the walls of the present cathedral had been erected, and, to prevent the property from becoming forfeited to the British Government, the lot and unfinished structure were deeded to Jesse Fish for one hundred dollars. The deed was a trust deed, and, upon the return of the Spaniards, the property was reconveyed by Mr. Fish to the Rev. Thomas Hassett, Vicar-General of Florida. The old parish church, which stood on the lot now belonging to the Episcopal parish, and west of their church edifice, had during the English possession been used as a courthouse. This old church was called "Our Lady of the Angels," and was built of stone, being probably the second church erected in the town by the Spaniards. The Spanish governor, immediately on taking possession, had fitted up this old church for worship, for which the second story was assigned, while on the first floor were rooms used for a guard, a temporary jail, and for storing provisions, all of which uses would seem more appropriate to the castle. Where the first wooden church stood I have been unable to learn, though there is some rather obscure evidence that it was near the present residence of Mr. Howard, on

St. George Street. How long the walls of the cathedral had been standing, before the change of flags, is unknown. In 1703 the king decreed an appropriation of $20,000 for the repair of the churches of St. Augustine injured by Colonel Daniel. In 1720 the crown sent $20,000 more, and in 1723 issued a decree to procure at once workmen and repair the convent, the church, and the walls of the city. In 1790 the king decreed the application of the rent from ten lots in Havana to finish the church. The inhabitants were urged to contribute in work or money; and it is said that they brought in poultry, which was very scarce, and donated the proceeds of the sales of their chickens, which then sold at a dollar apiece. The two old churches—"Nostra Senora de la Leche," and "Our Lady of the Angels"—were torn down, and the materials sold for the benefit of the new church, as well as such ornaments as were salable. From these sources it was reported to the Bishop of Cuba that the following amounts had been obtained: From the ornaments of the old churches, $3,978; from donations offered by "these wretched inhabitants," $850; the value of the stone in the two old and dilapidated churches, $800—a total of $5,628. To this amount the government applied revenues which amounted to $11,000. It was not long after the means were secured before the edifice was completed. It was blessed Dec. 8th, 1791. This new church, now called the cathedral, was constructed under the supervision of Don Mariana de la Roque, and presents a very pleasing architectural aspect. The front wall is carried above the roof, making a section of a bell-shaped cone, in excellent proportion and graceful curvature. The front entrance is supported by a circular arch, and upon each side stand two massive Doric columns supporting the entablature. The roof is supported by trusses, so that the whole auditorium is free from columns except two large stone pillars, which support the gallery immediately over the entrance, and thus form the vestibule. From the center of the ceiling hangs a unique chandelier, in which has been kept burning the sacred flame almost without intermission for nearly a hundred years. Near the vestibule, upon the left as you enter the church, is the sacred crucifix belonging to the early chapel of Nra. Sra. de la Leche. It is said that another ornament of this early chapel, a statue representing the blessed Virgin watching from the church over the camp of the new believers in her Son's divinity, is in the convent of St. Teresa, at Havana. A very interesting document is probably in the possession of the church in Cuba, which is an inventory taken under a decree, issued Feb. 6, 1764, by Morel, Bishop of Santa Cruz, enumerating all the ornaments, altars, effigies, bells, and jewels belonging to the churches and religious associations of St. Augustine. This inventory and much of the property was taken to Cuba in a schooner called *Our Lady of the Light*. From this record it might be possible to learn something of the history of the bells in the belfry of the cathedral. Of these there are four hanging in separate niches cut in the wall of the elevated front, three in niches having their floors upon the same plane, but the two outer ones are constructed of a less height than the center niche in which hangs the largest bell; the fourth is a small bell in a corresponding niche above the other three. I have always thought that one of these bells might have been used in the English church, though there is no record of it. The bell in the westerly niche, though the best in appearance, and having the brightest color, is probably the oldest bell upon this continent. The following inscription is cast upon its exterior surface :

SANCTE JOSEPH

ORA PRO NOBIS

D 1682

The other bells have inscriptions cast upon them, but no date. The small bell in the upper niche was placed there about fifty years ago, having been presented to the church by Don Geronimo Alverez, the same who was alcalde (mayor) when the monument was built. An interesting anecdote is told of this man, showing the power he possessed in the town. It is said that, soon after the change of flags, a funeral procession approached the church followed by pall-bearers decorated with a white sash, a custom then first introduced, which is still retained. At the entrance to the church they were met by this valiant but ignorant don, who fiercely brandished a staff, and declared that not one of the impious Freemasons should cross the threshold of the church except over his dead body. Argument was unavailing, and the ceremony at the church was necessarily dispensed with on that occasion, though the precaution was taken to inform the old gentleman, before the next funeral, that the sash was but a badge of mourning, and not the trappings of the devil.

The cathedral is one of the most ornamental and interesting structures in the town, and it is to be hoped that the revenues of the church may be sufficient to keep it in perfect preservation. At present it needs repairs.*

May 15th, 1792, the large barracks built by the British were burned. The lower story, only, was built of brick, the upper being of wood, while the porches on all sides were supported by stone pillars. After the destruction of these barracks, the Spanish governor made use of the convent of "The Conception of Our Lady," or St. Francis, as it was afterward called, for the accommodation of his troops. It has ever since been used for military purposes, though it still bears the canonized name Francis.

Finding that the Minorcans were unable to receive the full benefit from the teachings of the priests because of their inability to understand the Spanish language, the Vicar-General asked that there might be sent to St. Augustine a priest conversant with the language of this large proportion of his flock. In 1795, agreeably to this request, Friar McAfry Catalan, an Irish priest speaking the Minorcan language, arrived in St. Augustine. The Spanish governor, Don Juan Nepomuseno Quesada, made great efforts to settle the province, and allowed many extraordinary privileges, such as were not enjoyed in any other part of the Spanish dominions. In 1792 Florida was opened to general emigration without exception of country or creed. It was rapidly progressing to importance under this wise policy, when the Spanish Minister, growing jealous of the republican spirit of the new colonists, closed the gates against American citizens about the year 1804. Quesada, however, endeavored to procure a large Irish emigration, and wrote to Las Casas, Governor of Cuba, ask-

---

* A fine view of the cathedral, showing the four bells in the tower, and the ornamental front, is given in the Souvenir Album of Views in St. Augustine.

ing that the government would aid those of Irish nationality and Catholic faith to settle in the province. The governor replied that no settlers should be admitted to Florida unless they paid their own transportation and maintained themselves. He instructed Quesada to afford no other assistance than "lands, protection, good treatment, and no molestation in matters of religion, although there shall be no other public worship but Catholic." He also referred him to the "Law of the Indies." By this law lands were granted to new settlers, "making a distinction between gentlemen and peasants." A peasant's portion was a town lot fifty by one hundred feet—arable land, capable of producing one hundred fanegas (bushels) of wheat and ten of Indian corn, with as much land as two oxen can plow in a day for the raising of esculent roots; also pasture-land for eight breeding sows, twenty cows, five mares, one hundred sheep, and twenty goats.

A gentleman's portion was a lot in town one hundred by two hundred feet, and, of all the remainder, five times a peasant's portion. Many grants were made under this law by Governor Quesada, and the patents issued by him are the foundation of many titles of lands in the vicinity of St. Augustine.

At this time there were many customs, ordinances, and habits of life existing in this old town of which no record or chronicle now remains. One most respectable gentleman of the place has mentioned to the author that his mother was married to three different husbands in the space of two years. This would seem a very strange proceeding at the present day, but can be readily understood when we learn that, a hundred years ago, the women of this town were obliged to marry for protection. The following are some of the orders issued September 2d, 1790, by the Spanish governor: Order No. 12 prohibits all women under the age of forty (whether widows or single) from living otherwise than under the immediate protection of their parents or relations. Order No. 23 forbidding masters or supercargoes of vessels from selling their cargoes by wholesale without having first exposed the same for sale at retail eight days previously to the public. Order No. 25 prohibiting persons from galloping horses through the streets, and dogs from going at large except hounds and pointers. Order No. 27 prohibiting persons from walking the streets after nine o'clock at night without a lantern with a light therein. Another order prohibited the owners of billiard tables from admitting tradesmen, laborers, domestics, and boys on working days.

There were few events worth recording which happened under the Spanish rule after 1800, or at least that are of interest to the general reader. Just after the recession the Indians attacked the settlements, and burned Bella Vista, the country seat of Governor Moultrie, seven miles south of St. Augustine. These Indian contests continued during the whole succeeding period up to the change of flags, and were then transferred to the Americans. The Indians were in almost every instance incited by white men, or goaded to desperation by the deceptions of their white neighbors, who were ever attempting to either make slaves of the Indians or procure what negro slaves were owned by them. Just before the cession of Florida to the United States, there were said to be about a thousand Indians in the vicinity of St. Augustine. These obtained a living by hunting, raising herds of cattle, and crops of corn, and bringing wood into St. Augustine. This they were said to carry in bundles on their backs. About this time they were all nearly starved by the trickery of some unprincipled residents of St. Augustine. At the period when the attention of themselves and their negro slaves was directed to the cultivation of their crops a few worthless wretches, for the purpose of alarming the Indians, and inducing them to sell their slaves for almost nothing, went among the nation and spread the report that two thousand men under General Jackson were coming to expel them from their lands and carry away their slaves and cattle. This form of imposition had before proved successful, and did in this case. The Indians upon this abandoned their lands and sold their slaves, but before the next season experienced great suffering from want, while the unprincipled speculators having gratified their avarice were indifferent to the needs of the poor savages.

In January, 1811, President Monroe appointed George Matthews and John McKee commissioners, with power to occupy the Floridas with force, "should there be room to entertain a suspicion that a design existed in any other power to occupy the provinces." In pursuance of these instructions, which at this day must be considered simply extraordinary, one of the commissioners came to St. Augustine, and made a proposition to the Spanish governor to surrender the province to the United States, which was of course refused. Thereupon it was given out that the United States intended to occupy the province, and those whose interest would be served endeavored to bring such a result about by every means in their power. This was the period of the embargo in the United States. The port of Fernandina affording deep water, and a convenient point for shipping American productions, and being under the Spanish flag, became the resort for a large fleet of vessels. This was of course obnoxious to the United States authorities, who offered every encouragement to a large class of citizens who were anxious to escape from the Spanish rule.

In March, 1812, a large number of these individuals organized a provisional government, and soon after, with the help of Commodore Campbell, United States Navy, obtained the capitulation of the town and fort on Amelia Island. Still encouraged, and led by citizens and officers of the United States, these men, styling themselves patriots, began a march toward St. Augustine, and taking possession of the old Fort Mosa, invested the place. From this place they were dislodged by a Spanish gun-boat, but they still hovered about the town and cut off all supplies. It is said that the courage and activity of a company of negroes commanded by a free black, named Prince, alone saved the people of the town from starvation. At this period a barrel of corn sold for sixteen dollars. At the same time the Indians were urged to attack the Americans and "patriots," and for the space of a year there was a constant strife between these parties throughout Florida. In May, 1813, President Monroe, seeing that he had gone too far in incroaching upon the territory of a friendly nation, withdrew the American troops from Florida. These incursions under American protection in East Florida, like General Jackson's unhesitating course in attacking the British on Spanish territory in West Florida, plainly showed the King of Spain how precarious and unreliable was the tenure of his sovereignty. The Spanish nation had held the territory of Florida for two hundred and fifty years, constantly yielding to the French and English portions adjacent originally claimed by Spain. The great hopes of wealth and a vast revenue from the province had never been realized; but, on the contrary, vast outlays had constantly been required, which were supplied by the more prosperous provinces and the home government. In 1811, Governor Estrada writes to the Captain-General of Cuba, that the $140,013 and 4 reals allowed annually for salaries was urgently needed ; also that there were no funds wherewith to pay "the annual presents of the Indians, the payments due invalids, Florida pensioners and settlers, who receive a daily pension and charity, whose outcries are so continual that the most obdurate heart would melt at them with compassion."

Under these circumstances it was but natural that the King of Spain should be willing to rid himself of this so very unprofitable province. The United States, upon the other hand, were anxious to obtain the possession of the peninsula to complete their coast line.

In 1819 a treaty of amity was concluded between his Catholic Majesty and the United States, whereby the two Floridas were ceded to the latter power as an indemnity for damages estimated at five million dollars. This treaty was dated February 22d, 1819, and ratified February 22d, 1821.

Seven years before the cession the Spanish Cortes had issued an order to the authorities of all the Spanish colonies to erect in some public place of their principal town a monument as a memorial of the liberal constitution which had been granted to Spain and her provinces. Accordingly, the City Council of St. Augustine, probably with the crown's funds, erected upon the public square a monument to commemorate a grant of the privilege of representation, which the people of the province never even asked for, much less enjoyed. At the east end of the public square, or "Plaza de la Constitucion," as it is now called, there stood, in Spanish times, the government drug store, two private houses used as dwellings, a bar-room, and the town market. Adjoining the market was a bell-tower, and the guard in front of the public jail, which stood where the St. Augustine Hotel now is, used to strike the bell in the tower to mark the hours, which were counted with the old-fashioned sand-glass standing within the tower under the supervision of the guard. As these buildings occupied about a fourth part of the present plaza, the monument, though now situated toward the western side of the square, then stood in the center of the inclosure. Soon after its completion, the Spanish government issued orders that all monuments erected to the constitution throughout its realms should be razed. The citizens of St. Augustine were much grieved to think of losing their monument, which was considered a great ornament to the public park, and appealed to the governor and principal men to allow the decree to be disregarded. It was finally decided to allow the monument to stand without the inscription. The citizens accordingly removed the marble tablets upon which the inscriptions had been engraved, and placed them in concealment, where they remained until 1818, when they were restored without opposition. This monument is the only one in existence commemorative of the Spanish constitution of 1812. It is twenty feet high, standing upon a foundation of granite with a square pedestal, from which the shaft rises in a curve, and thence tapers with rectilinear surfaces to its top, which is surmounted by a cannon-ball. It is constructed of coquina, and its surface is cemented and kept whitewashed, except the ball upon the summit, which is painted black. Don Geronimo Alvarez was alcalde at the time it was erected. Upon three of the four sides there is set in the masonry a small marble tablet bearing the inscription, "Plaza de la Constitucion." Upon the east side is the large marble tablet upon which is engraved the following:

*Plaza de la
Constitucion.
Promulga en esta Ciudad
de San Agustin de la Florida
Oriental en 17 de Octubre de
1812 siendo Gobernador el
Brigadier Don Sebastian
Kindalem Cuba Here
del order de Santiago.
Peira eterna memoria
El Ayuntamiento Consti-
tucional Erigioeste Obelisco
dirigido por Don Fer-
nando de la Plaza**
Arredondo el Joven
Regidor De cano y
Don Franciscor Robira
Procurador Sindico.
Año de 1813*

TRANSLATION.

Plaza of the Constitution, promulgated in the city of St. Augustine, East Florida, on the 17th day of October, the year 1812. Being then Governor the Brigadier Don Sebastian Kindalem, Knight of the order of San Diego.

FOR ETERNAL REMEMBRANCE,

the Constitutional City Council erected this monument under the supervision of Don Fernando de la Maza Arredondo, the young

---

* Maza, engraver's mistake.

municipal officer, oldest member of the corporation, and Don Franciscor Robira, Attorney and Recorder.

Immediately under the date there is cut in the marble tablet the Masonic emblem of the square and compass. The reader can readily believe that the City Council of St. Augustine in 1813 were all too good Catholics to be responsible for this symbol of Masonry. The history of that piece of vandalism is said to be as follows: Soon after the close of the war of the Rebellion, the "young bloods" amused themselves by endeavoring to create an alarm in the mind of the United States commandant, and, by executing a series of cabalistic marks at different localities throughout the town, to convey the impression that a secret society was in existence, and about to do some act contrary to the peace and dignity of the United States. Besides other marks and notices posted upon private and public buildings about the town this square and compass was one night cut upon the tablet of the Spanish monument, where it will remain as long as the tablet exists, an anomaly, without this explanation.

CHAPTER XVII.

FLORIDA CEDED TO THE UNITED STATES.—ATTEMPT OF THE SPANISH GOVERNOR TO CARRY AWAY THE RECORDS.—DESCRIPTION OF ST. AUGUSTINE WHEN TRANSFERRED.—POPULATION IN 1830.—TOWN DURING THE INDIAN WAR.—OSCEOLA AND COA-COU-CHE.—A TRUE ACCOUNT OF THE DUNGEON IN THE OLD FORT, AND THE IRON CAGES.—THE INDIANS BROUGHT TO ST. AUGUSTINE IN 1875.

EAST FLORIDA was delivered by Governor Coppinger to Lieut. Rob. Butler, U. S. A., on the 10th of July, 1821. It had been intended to have the transfer take place on the anniversary of the declaration of American Independence; but the Spaniards, feeling no particular regard for the 4th of July, made no efforts to hasten the settlement of the preliminaries, and were therefore unprepared to turn over the province until the tenth of the month.

On the 30th of March, 1822, Congress passed an act incorporating into a territory the two Floridas, and authorizing a legislative council and a superior court, which were to meet alternately at Pensacola and St. Augustine. William P. Duval was appointed the first governor, to hold his office for three years. It is an interesting fact that among those who were saved with Laudonnère at the massacre of the French Huguenots was one "Francis Duval of Rouen, son of him of the Iron Crown of Rouen."

General Jackson had been compelled to imprison the Spanish governor of West Florida for refusing to deliver certain papers that were considered indispensable. Fearing that the attempt would be made by the Governor of East Florida to carry away papers which should be delivered with the territory, General Jackson sent Captain J. R. Hanham from Pensacola to demand such papers and records as properly belonged to the Americans after the change of flags. Captain Hanham made the journey across the State—a distance of 600 miles—in seventeen days. He arrived none too soon, as the vessel was then in the harbor upon which it was intended to send papers and archives sufficient to fill eleven large boxes. After Governor Coppinger had refused to deliver these, Captain Hanham forced a room in the government house and seized the boxes, which had already been packed with the papers ready for shipment. Other valuable papers were shipped and lost on the passage to Havana, some say destroyed by pirates, others by the wreck of the vessel.

In 1823 St. Augustine witnessed for the second time the assembly of a legislative body, the second session of the territorial council being held that year in the government house. In the same year a treaty was concluded at Moultrie Creek, seven miles south of the city, with the Indian tribes of Florida, in which they agreed to surrender all their lands in the territory. It is needless to say that this treaty was never executed.

Forbes's "Sketches," published the year of the cession, gives an interesting account of the condition of St. Augustine at the end of the Spanish possession. It is related in these words: "The town, built in Spanish manner, forms an oblong square, or parallelogram; the streets are regularly laid out, but the buildings have not been put up to conform strictly to that rule. The streets are generally so narrow as to admit with difficulty carriages to pass each other. To make up for this inconvenience they have a terrace foundation, and, being shaded, renders the walking very agreeable. The houses are built generally of a freestone peculiar to the country, which, with the aid of an outer coat of plaster, has a handsome and durable effect. They are only two stories high, thick walls with spacious entries, large doors, windows, and balconies, and a garden lot to each, more commonly stocked with orange and fig trees, interspersed with grape-vines and flowers. On entering this old town from the sea, the grandeur of the Castle of Fort St. Mark's presents itself, and imposes a degree of respect upon travelers upon seeing a fort forty feet high, in the modern taste of military architecture, commanding the entrance. The works are bronzed and squamated by age, but will, with some American ingenuity, be justly deemed one of the handsomest in the western hemisphere. It mounts sixty guns of twenty-four pounds, of which sixteen are bronze, and is calculated to contain one thousand men for action ; with which, and the courage such a fort should inspire, it is capable of a noble defense, having in old times resisted some formidable attacks. It is not liable to be shattered by balls, nor does it expose its defenders to the fatal effects of storms [stormings]. From the castle, southward, are the remains of a stone wall trenching its glacis, built to prevent the incroachment of the sea ; along this is a very pleasant walk as far as the market-place, which is opposite the old Government House in the center of the town, and separated from it by an oblong square called the parade, on which there is a Roman Catholic church of modern construction and quite ornamental. In front of this there formerly stood a handsome and spacious edifice, built in modern style by Lieut.-Governor Moultrie for a State-house, which was not completed. For want of an exterior coat of plaster it has crumbled to pieces, leaving not a single vestige of its former splendor.

"The old Government House, now much decayed, is occupied as a barrack for the Royal Artillery. It leaves the marks of a heavy pile of buildings in the Spanish style, having balconies in front, galleries and areas on both sides, with several irregular additions well contrived for the climate. Among these was an outlook built by Governor Grant, on the western summit of the main building, which commanded a full view of the sea-coast and surrounding country. The garden attached to the Government House is surrounded by a stone wall; it was formerly laid out with great taste, and stocked with most of the exotic and indigenous plants common to the tropics and the Middle States, such as the pomegranate, plantain, pineapple, papau, olive, and sugarcane. The orange and lemon trees here grow to large size, and produce better fruit than they do in Spain and Portugal.

"From the square environed by orange trees the streets extend southwardly to some stone buildings, one of which was formerly a Franciscan convent, now converted into a jail, but under the British was used as barracks. In addition they constructed the very large and handsome buildings, four stories high, of wood, with materials brought from New York and intended for Pensacola, but detained by Governor Grant. These barracks at the southern extremity of the peninsula in which the town is built formed an elegant appendage to it, but were burned and now exhibit only the stack of chimneys. In a course westward from these vestiges of royalty are streets leading to a bridge formerly of wood but now of stone, crossing a small creek running parallel with the sea, on the east side, and St. Sebastian on the west. Over this are several valuable and highly improved orange groves and several redoubts, forming the south and western lines of fortification. Near the bridge, in the same street as the Government House, is the burying-ground of the Protestants, where stood an Episcopal church with a handsome steeple, not a vestige of which remains.

"Before the entrance of some of the houses built by the Spaniards rises a portico of stone arches, the roofs of which are commonly flat. There are nearly one thousand houses of all descriptions in the town, which is about three-quarters of a mile in length by one-quarter in breadth. As it is built upon a point of land it is in some degree insulated by the conflux of Matanzas River and St. Sebastian Creek, by which means the egress by land must be by the northern gates, and by a bridge and causeway in a western direction. The whole forms a very picturesque piece of scenery, being surrounded by orange groves and kitchen gardens. Within the first line [of redoubts upon the north] was a small settlement of Germans, with a church of their own, on St. Mark's River: within the same was an Indian town, with a church also; but it must be regretted that nothing of these remains, as they serve if not as temples certainly as ornamental relics.

"The governor has given the land belonging to this township as glebe land to the parish church, which will no doubt be confirmed by the American Government in its liberal appropriations for religious purposes. The harbor of St. Augustine would be one of the best in the world were it not for the bar, which admits vessels drawing not more than six feet with safety. It is surrounded by breakers which are not as dangerous as they appear. There is a roadstead on the north side of the bar with good anchorage for vessels drawing too much water to enter the harbor. [A part of Anastatia Island] is known as Fish's Island, and from the hospitality of Mr. Jesse Fish, one of the oldest inhabitants of the province, is remarkable for the date and olive trees, the flavor of the oranges, and the cultivation of his garden." *

The location of the Protestant cemetery as here described is confusing, being located near "this bridge, in the same street as the Government House." Probably the text should read, in the same street as the Convent House, which would place the Episcopal church and cemetery near the southern end of St. George Street.

Another account, published about the same period as Forbes's, gives the following picture of the town: "Somewhat more than half way between the fort and the south end of the western peninsula a stone causeway and wooden bridge crosses Mari-Sanchez (Santa Maria) Creek, and connects the two portions or precincts of the town. It is to the north of this causeway that the principal part of the buildings are placed, forming a parallelogram somewhat more than a quarter of a mile wide from east to west, and three-quarters in length from north to south. The neck of land (on which the town is built) is divided into two peninsulas by Mari-Sanchez (Santa Maria) Creek, running parallel to the harbor, but heading in some low lands within the lines. It is on the eastern peninsula alone that the town is built, the western one being occupied by kitchen gardens, corn fields, orange groves, and pasture grounds. The houses on the side of the harbor are chiefly of stone, having only one story above the ground floor: these latter are invariably laid with a coat of tabia, a mixture of sand and shells, and are scarcely ever used but as store rooms, the families living in the upper stories.†

---

* Forbes's Sketches, pp. 85 to 89.

† From inquiry of the old inhabitants I do not find this statement confirmed. Perhaps the richer class of people made no use of the ground floors, but the general custom was to use them as is still done.

"The dwellings on the back streets with few exceptions, particularly in the north-west quarter, have but the ground floor, and are generally built of wood, though stone ones are common, but almost all are laid with tabia flooring."*

At the census of 1830 St. Augustine and environs contained four thousand inhabitants, of whom eight hundred and forty-four were free blacks. The large number of free persons of color is accounted for by the fact that St. Augustine under the Spanish had been an asylum for all the runaway slaves from the neighboring colonies. They had been formed into a military company, and after the "patriot war" of 1812 to 1816 lands had been donated to them for their services. It was also said that those born in the province were registered from their birth, and a severe penalty imposed upon any master of a vessel who should attempt to carry any of them away.

In 1822 an attempt was made to deprive the Roman Catholics of the cathedral. A petition of the inhabitants was thereupon presented to Congress, and that body passed an act on February 8, 1827, granting and confirming to the Catholic society of St. Augustine the building and grounds where they now worship.

In 1821 Rev. Andrew Fowler, a missionary from Charleston, South Carolina, organized the present Episcopal parish. The corner-stone of the present church edifice was laid by the Rev. Edward Phillips on the 23d of June, 1825, and the building was consecrated by Bishop Bowen of South Carolina in the year 1833. The church is a small and plain structure, but in very good taste, and ornamented with a steeple. It is built of coquina, and from its location fronting the plaza, is one of the most noticeable buildings in the city.

---

* Vignole's History.

The Presbyterian church, though built later, 1830, has a less modern appearance. This church, which was fitted in quite the old-fashioned style, with high-backed pews facing the entrance doors between which was the pulpit, underwent a remodeling of the interior in 1879.

By act of Congress dated March 30, 1823, East and West Florida were united as one territory. Florida was admitted into the Union as a State, March 3d, 1845.

In 1830 there was quite a spirit of speculation rife in the old city. A canal into the St. Johns River and another between the Halifax and Matanzas rivers, also a railway to Picolata were projected, and sanguine people fully expected to see these projects completed immediately. To this day the railway alone has been completed, and is barely able to pay a dividend to its stockholders with a tariff of two dollars for a carriage of fifteen miles. All the other projects are still being talked of.

One of the bubbles of the speculation of this period was a new and large city to be built north of the fort. Peter Sken Smith, a gentleman of some means, erected the frame of a large hotel on grounds outside of the city gate, and there were also built there several houses and stores, a market, and a wharf. Judge Douglass, the first judge of the territory, entered largely into the business of raising the silk-worm. He set out a large number of mulberry trees and built a large building on his plantation called Macarasi, or more commonly Macariz, situated just beyond the end of the shell road, which gave to the place the general appellation of the "Cocoonery." Judge Douglass has been ridiculed for yielding to the "silk-growing fever," but the enterprise which was so disastrous to him and others will one day become a lucrative business for many in the mild climate of Florida.

The large and handsome residence on the lot adjoining the Episcopal church, now owned by L. H. Tyler, Esq., was built by Peter Sken Smith, in 1833. The artisans and much of the materials were brought from the North, and the sum of forty thousand dollars was said to have been invested on the house and furniture. Shortly after the house was for sale at less than two thousand dollars.

The plaza was inclosed about this time, and the cannon placed at the corners. The old guns yet to be seen about the city were used by several private citizens to ornament the corners of the streets upon which their lots fronted. In a cut published thirty years ago showing the plaza, etc., the date-palms in Mr. Tyler's yard appear to reach to an altitude almost the same as at present, showing the extreme slowness of their upward growth.

St. Augustine, immediately after it came under the jurisdiction of the United States, began to receive a most desirable addition to its population in a class of Americans of culture and means, who had long desired to avail themselves of the benefits and delights of its climate, but had hesitated about becoming citizens of the place under Spanish rule. I have heard old citizens say that there was no town of its size in the country where there were so many persons of refined tastes and independent means as in St. Augustine at that time. The Indian war soon after brought to St. Augustine a large addition to its population. This consisted mostly of the military, both regulars and militia, of Florida and the neighboring States, and the many officers, agents, and attachés of the government. It was the government headquarters and a depot of supplies, and for a season was full of bustle, excitement, and more activity than it has ever experienced since.

The incidents of that war would be out of place in a history of

St. Augustine. Two of the principal characters of that exciting time were, however, brought to St. Augustine, and, with about three hundred other Creeks and Seminoles, confined in Fort Marion. Osceola, a young chief of the Mickasookie tribe, of great daring, considerable education, and great natural abilities, inherited with the Caucasian blood derived from his father, was for some time confined at St. Augustine, and afterwards removed to Fort Moultrie, in Charleston Harbor, where his body is now buried. Though captured through a base trick, Osceola had, through a sullen sense of honor, refused to escape from Fort Marion with Wild Cat. It was said that he died of a broken heart when he learned the fate of his nation, and the intention of the government to remove the remnant of the Seminoles west of the Mississippi.

The casemate in the south-west bastion of the fort has been rendered famous by the escape of a body of Indians, including the famous Coa-cou-che. This Indian, also called Wild Cat, was the youngest son of Philip, a great chief among the Seminoles. He was a man of great courage, of an adventurous disposition, and savage nature, lacking the intellectual abilities of Osceola, but possessing great influence among his nation. Like most of the young chiefs, he was bitterly opposed to the execution of the treaty signed by the older chiefs, by which the Seminoles agreed to remove west of the Mississippi. At an interview immediately before the breaking out of hostilities, Colonel Harney observed to him that unless the Seminoles removed according to the treaty the whites would exterminate them. To this Coa-cou-che replied, that Iste-chatte (the Indian) did not understand that word. The Great Spirit he knew might exterminate them, but the pale-faces could not; else, why had they not done it before?

During the war this young chief was captured and placed under guard in Fort Marion. It is reported that he was at first confined in one of the close cells, and, in order to be removed to a casemate which had an embrasure through which he had planned to escape, he complained of the dampness of his cell and feigned sickness. This, like many other incidents connected with his escape, is probably fictitious. There were at the time a considerable number of Indians confined in the fort, and unless they showed themselves querulous and dangerous, they were all allowed the freedom of the court during the day, and confined at night in the several casemates. It is probable that Coa-cou-che chose the casemate in the south-west bastion from which to make his escape, because of a platform which is in that casemate. This platform is raised some five feet from the floor, and built of masonry directly under the embrasure through which he escaped. This opening had been constructed high up in the outer wall of the casemate to admit light and air. It is thirteen feet above the floor, and eight feet above the platform, which had probably been constructed for the convenience and dignity of the judges, who doubtless used this casemate as a judgment room. The aperture is about two feet high by nine inches wide, and some eighteen feet above the surface of the ground at the foot of the wall within the moat. It is said that as he took his airing upon the terre-plein the evening before his escape, Coa-cou-che lingered longer than usual, gazing far out into the west as the sun went down, probably thinking that ere another sunset he would be beyond the limit of his farthest vision, enjoying the freedom of his native forests. That night he squeezed his body, said to have been attenuated by voluntary abstinence from food, through the embrasure in the wall, and silently dropped into the moat at the foot of the bastion. The moat was dry, and the station of every guard was well known to the Indian, so that escape was no longer difficult. Coa-cou-che immediately joined his nation, but was afterwards captured and sent west. He was recalled by General Worth, and used to secure the submission of his tribe. General Worth declared to him that if his people were not at Tampa on a certain day he would hang from the yard of the vessel on which he had returned, and was then confined. This message he was ordered to send to his people by Indian runners furnished by the general. He was directed to deliver to the messengers twenty twigs, one for each day, and to make it known to his people that when the last twig in the hands of the messenger was broken, so would the cords which bound his life to earth be snapped asunder unless they were all at the general's camp prepared to depart to the reservation provided for them at the west. The struggle in the mind of Coa-cou-che was severe, but his love of life was strong. He sent by the messenger his entreaties that his people should appear at the time and place designated, and take up their abode in the prairies of the west. Desiring to impress upon his people that this was the will of the Great Spirit, with consummate policy he directed the messenger to relate to them this, Coa-cou-che's dream : '' The day and manner of my death are given out so that whatever I may encounter, I fear nothing. The spirits of the Seminoles protect me ; and the spirit of my twin-sister who died many years ago watches over me ; when I am laid in the earth I shall go to live with her. She died suddenly. I was out hunting, and when seated by my campfire alone I heard a strange noise—a voice that told me to go to her. The camp was some distance off, but I took my wife and started. The night was dark and gloomy ; the wolves howled about me. I went from hommock to hommock, sounds came often to my ear. I thought she was speaking to me. At daylight I reached the camp, but she was dead. I sat down alone under the long gray moss of the trees, when I heard strange sounds again. I felt myself moving, and went along into a new country where all was bright and beautiful. I saw clear water ponds, rivers, and prairies upon which the sun never set. All was green; the grass grew high, and the deer stood in the midst looking at me. I then saw a small white cloud approaching, and when just before me, out of it came my twin-sister dressed in white, and covered with bright silver ornaments. Her long black hair which I had often braided fell down upon her back. She clasped me around the neck and said, 'Coa-cou-che, Coa-cou-che.' I shook with fear; I knew her voice, but could not speak. With one hand she gave me a string of white beads; in the other she held a cup sparkling with pure water; as I drank she sang the peace song of the Seminoles, and danced around me. She had silver bells upon her feet which made a loud sweet noise. Taking from her bosom something, she laid it before me, when a bright blaze streamed above us. She took me by the hand and said, 'All is peace.' I wanted to ask for others, but she shook her head, stepped into the cloud, and was gone. All was silent. I felt myself sinking until I reached the earth when I met my brother, Chilka." *

Coa-cou-che's appeal was successful. The messengers returned with the whole remnant of the tribe three days before the expiration of the time. They all embarked and took up their residence on the prairies, where the sun never sets and the grass grows high. It was not a field in which Coa-cou-che could dis-

---

* Sprague's History of the Seminole War.

tinguish himself, and from this time his name was never heard, except in connection with his past exploits in Florida.

Soon after the United States took possession of St. Augustine, the government began to make extensive improvements in and about the town. The barracks were immediately remodeled, and built as they are at present. The fort, which had become much dilapidated, was repaired and fitted for a garrison. It was while this work was being prosecuted that the cell under the north-east bastion was discovered, which has ever since been associated with the Huguenot massacre and the Spanish Inquisition, in annual editions of guide-books and tourists' letters. It is constantly designated as "the Dungeon," and, lest I should not be understood in referring to it as a cell, I shall also call it a dungeon, in explaining how it was found and what it did not contain. For some reason unexplained by any record left by the Spaniards, the terre-plein, near the north-east bastion, had been built upon large wooden beams. At the time the Americans took possession of the fort they found the last casemate, fronting on the court on the east side, filled with the coquina floor of the terre-plein, which had fallen in, as the timbers supporting it had rotted. Naturally, this half-filled casemate had become the place of deposit for all rubbish accumulated upon any part of the works. In the course of repairs the rubbish was cleared out of the casemate, and the entrance into the adjoining cell exposed. Entering this cell, and examining the masonry for anticipated repairs, the engineer in charge, said to be Lieutenant Tuttle, U. S. A., discovered a newness of appearance about a small portion of the masonry of the north wall. Under his instruction a mason cut out this newer stone-work and found that the small arch, under which those who now enter the "dungeon" crawl, had been walled up. Why the entrance had thus been filled with masonry is unknown, but it is extremely unlikely that it was done to insure the perpetual captivity and death of a human being. The engineer and mason entered the cell, and made an examination of the interior with the light of a candle. Near the entrance were the remains of a fire, the ashes and bits of pine wood burned off toward the center of the pile in which they had been consumed. Upon the side of the cell was a rusty staple, with about three links of chain attached thereto. Near the wall, on the west side of the cell, were a few bones. Finding these very rotten, and crumbling to pieces under his touch, the engineer spread his handkerchief upon the floor and brushed very gently the few fragments of bone into it. These were shown the surgeon then stationed at the post, who said they might be human bones, but were so badly crumbled and decayed he could not determine definitely. Nothing else was found in the cell.* The iron cages, which have been described as a part of the fixtures of this terrible dungeon, and which it has been said contained human bones, appear upon the united testimony of old inhabitants to have been found outside of the city gates entirely empty. It is said that, in 1822, a Mr. Deever, a butcher, while digging post holes on the grounds opposite to those now owned by Mr. Kingsland, just north of the city gates, came upon the cages and dug them up. One of them was made use of in his workshop by Mr. Bartolo Oliveros, a locksmith. The other one was allowed by Mr. Deever to lie near the city gate until it was appropriated by some unknown party. The cages are described as having had much the

---

* The finding of any bones is denied by Major H. W. Benham, U. S. A., on the authority of a Mr. Ridgely, Lieutenant Tuttle's overseer. Major Benham took charge of the work upon the fort in January, 1839.

shape of a coffin ; and the tradition is, that a human being had been placed in each, the solid bands of iron riveted about his body, and, after life had been extinguished by the horrible torture of starvation, cages and corpses had been buried in the "scrub" then covering the ground north of the gate. Doubtless these cages were used for the punishment of criminals condemned for some heinous crime ; but whether they were introduced by the Spaniards or English is not known. An old gentleman, Mr. Christobal Bravo, tells me his mother has related to him that she had seen, during the English possession, these cages, or similar ones, suspended at the gates of the city, with criminals incarcerated therein. In the face of the facts it is feared that St. Augustine must lose much of the romance and melancholy interest excited by the stories of Spanish cruelty and torture. It is very probable that this inner cell at the fort was used as a place of confinement for criminals, and it is possible that some may have died therein. In fact, it was so reported and generally believed at the time the poet Bryant visited St. Augustine in 1843. Fairbanks, on page 157 of his "History and Antiquities of St. Augustine," published in 1858, refers to the instruments of torture and skeletons walled in the old fort.

The account, as recited by the "Old Sergeant," Mr. McGuire, ordnance-sergeant, U. S. A., gives the current legend connected with the dungeon. The sergeant alone can do justice to the narrative, in presence of an appreciative audience clustered around his smoking torch under the vaulted arch of the grim, damp cell. No pen can transcribe the sergeant's Irish brogue, or his periods, his tones, and his inimitable expression of countenance, which seems to evince a combination of honest doubt and wishful credence in the melancholy tale of Spanish barbarity, which has proved so remunerative to himself, and so acceptable to the novelty hunting tourist. While the sergeant's lamp holds out to burn, no visitor to St. Augustine should fail to hear his tale, "Just as it was told to me," as he is particular to explain.

In the spring of 1875 a body of Comanche, Kiowa, and Cheyenne chiefs were removed from the West by order of the government, and sent to St. Augustine. These Indians were, at first, confined within the old fort, under a guard furnished from the post at St. Francis Barracks. They had been sent under the charge of Captain Pratt, of the Tenth U. S. Cavalry. The selection of this officer was a most fortunate choice. Through his indubitable faith in the possibility of developing the better nature of the Indian, together with his unwearied perseverance under difficulties that none but a missionary among the depraved races of men can realize, by his great tact and his patience he succeeded in demonstrating that, by proper methods and efforts, the Indian problem is capable of a satisfactory solution. Under the system adopted by Captain Pratt the guard was soon dispensed with, and the Indians treated very much as if they were a company of enlisted soldiers. They walked the streets, attended the churches, and had their school, with no other restraint or hindrance than is imposed upon soldiers. They soon acted as their own guard day and night, assumed the dress of a soldier, and many of the manners and habits of the white man. After remaining at St. Augustine for about two years, a portion of the company were sent to the Hampton, Va., school, and the remainder were returned to their native tribes, where they must yet exert a powerful influence for the advance of civilization.

It is a remarkable coincidence that the first practical demonstration of the ability of the government to elevate and civilize the Indian, and the first advance in a rational method of making citizens of the remnant of our aboriginal population, was inaugurated at St. Augustine. The evil in the nature of the Caucasian who first landed in America, upon the shores of Florida, has proved a curse and a blight to the red man. The gratifying success that crowned the philanthropic policy inaugurated by the government among the representatives of the Indian race, while prisoners at St. Augustine, will, it is to be hoped, be the harbinger of the speedy civilization of the whole of the Indian race existing in America.

CHAPTER XVIII.

ST. AUGUSTINE AS IT USED TO BE.—CUSTOMS.—THE OLDEST STRUCTURE IN THE UNITED STATES.—PRESENT POPULATION.—OBJECTS OF INTEREST.—BUILDINGS ANCIENT AND MODERN.—ST. AUGUSTINE DURING THE REBELLION.—CLIMATE.—ADVANTAGES AS A HEALTH RESORT.

IN February, 1835, an unprecedented depression of temperature destroyed the orange trees which embosomed the town and rendered the place exceedingly attractive. The deep green foliage concealed the dingy and often unsightly buildings. The fragrance of the blossoms in spring was almost overpowering, and was said to be perceptible far out to sea. The income of the people of the town derived from the sale of their oranges was not far from seventy-five thousand dollars annually, and the crop that was yearly sent from St. Augustine in sailing vessels exceeded three million oranges. One orange tree upon the plaza is reported to have borne twelve thousand oranges. In 1829, Mr. A. Alverez picked from one tree in his garden six thousand five hundred oranges, and it is recorded that "an old citizen picked from one tree eight thousand of the golden apples. The Minorcan population of St. Augustine had been accustomed to depend on the produce of their little groves of eight or ten trees, to purchase their coffee, sugar, and other necessaries from the stores; they were left without resource. The wild groves suffered equally with those cultivated. The town of St. Augustine, that heretofore appeared like a rustic village, its white houses peeping from the clustered boughs and golden fruit of their favorite tree, beneath whose shade the foreign invalid cooled his fevered limbs, and imbibed health from the fragrant air, how is she fallen! Dry, unsightly poles, with ragged bark, stick up around her dwellings, and where the mocking bird once delighted to build her nest, and tune her lovely song, owls now hoot at night, and sterile winds whistle through the leafless branches. Never was a place more desolate."*

Many of the trees had attained a very large size and great age. A large number sent out sprouts from the roots, and if undisturbed, many groves would have borne profitable crops in a few years. The scale insect, however, made its appearance in 1842 in countless multitudes, blighting the groves throughout Florida. For twenty years it was a constant struggle, on the part of the few who retained their faith in the success of orange culture, to rid their groves of this destructive insect. Finally, nature provided in some way an exterminator of the insect, and from that time there has been no serious drawback to the culture of oranges in Florida. Williams describes the inhabitants at this time as "a temperate, quiet, and rather indolent people; affectionate and friendly to each other, and kind to the few slaves they held. They mostly kept little stores, cultivated small groves or gardens, and followed fishing and hunting." Posey balls, masquerades, and sherivarees were their principal diversions.

The posey dance of St. Augustine was introduced in the following manner: "The females of a family, no matter what their rank or station in life may be, erect in a room of their house a

---

* Williams's History, page 18.

neat little altar, lit up with candles, and dressed with pots and festoons of flowers. This is understood by the gentlemen as a polite invitation to call and admire the taste of the fair architects. It is continued for several successive evenings; in the meantime the lady selects from her visitors some happy beau, whom she delights to honor, and presents him with a bouquet of choice flowers. His gallantry is then put to the test; should he choose to decline the proffered honor, he has only to pay the expenses of lighting up the altar. But if he accepts the full dignity offered him, he is king of the ball, which shortly succeeds, and the posey lass becomes queen, as a matter of course. The posey ball is a mixed assembly. People of all ranks meet here on a level, yet they are conducted with the nicest decorum, and even with politeness and grace.

Sherivarees are parties of idle people, who dress themselves in grotesque masquerade, whenever a widow or widower is married. They often parade about the streets and play buffoon tricks for two or three days; haunting the residence of the new married pair, and disturbing the whole city with noise and riot.

The carnival is a scene of masquerading, which was formerly celebrated by the Spanish and Minorcan populations with much taste and gayety; but since the introduction of an American population, it has during the whole winter season been prostituted to cover drunken revels, and to pass the basest objects of society into the abodes of respectable people, to the great annoyance of the civil part of the community."*

These and other customs have long since ceased to exist, and many are already forgotten. One of these was "shooting the

---

* Williams's History, pp. 115 et seq.

Jews," originally a religious ceremony, but afterwards a diversion. For many years it was the custom to hang effigies at the street corners and upon the plaza on the evening of Good Friday. When the bells in the cathedral, which are never rung during Good Friday, began on Saturday morning at ten o'clock to ring the Hallelujah, crowds of men in the streets commenced to shoot with guns and pistols at the hanging effigies. This was continued until some unerring marksman severed the cord about the neck of the image, or perhaps it was riddled and shredded by the fusilade.

The Spanish veil was until a late period the only covering for the head worn by the ladies of the town. A lady now living has described the disapproval manifested at the appearance of the first bonnet in church. Great indignation was expressed, and loud protests against the insult offered to the church and congregation by this supposed exhibition of ill-breeding and irreverence.

In the memory of those now living wheeled vehicles within the gates were first allowed. Before that time all moving of goods was done in packs. The narrow streets without sidewalks evidently were not intended for the passage of carts and carriages. Saddle-horses were common, but their path was the center of the street, which was rendered hard and smooth with pounded coquina, and kept so neat that the ladies wore on their feet only the thinnest of slippers.

One of the ancient customs brought from the island of Minorca is yet continued.

On the night before Easter Sunday the young men go about the city in parties serenading. Approaching the dwelling of some one whom they wish to favor with their song, or from whom they expect the favors asked in their rhyme, they knock gently upon the window. If their visit is welcome they are answered by a knock from within, and at once begin the following song said to be in the Mahonese dialect:

	[TRANSLATION.]
"US GOIS.	"THE STANZAS.

"Disciarem lu dol
Cantarem aub' alagria,
Y n'arem a dá
Las pascuas a Maria.
    O Maria!

"Let us leave off mourning,
Let us sing with joy,
Let us go and give
Our salutation to Mary.
    O Mary!

"San Gabriel
Qui portaba la ambasciada
Des nostro rey del cel,
Estaran vos preñada.
Ya omitiada
Tuao vais aqui serventa,
Fia del Deo contenta,
Para fa lo que el vol.
    Disciarem lu dol, etc.

"Saint Gabriel
Brought the tidings
That the King of Heaven
Thou hadst conceived.
Thou wert humble.
Behold, here is the handmaid,
Daughter of God, content
To do what he will!
    CHORUS.—Let us leave off mourning, etc.

"Y a milla nit
Pariguero vos regina—
A un Deo infinit—
Dintra una establina.
Y a milla dia,
Que los angels von cantant
Par y abondant,
De la gloria de Deo sol.
    Disciarem lu dol, etc.

"And at midnight
She gave birth to the child—
The infinite God—
In a stable.
At mid-day,
The angels go singing
Peace and abundance,
And glory to God alone.
    CHORUS.

"Y a Libalem,
Alla la terra santa,
Nus nat Jesus,
Aub' alagria tanta;
Infant petit
Que tot lu mon salvaria.
Y ningu y bastaria
Nu mes un Deo sol.
    Disciarem lu dol, etc.

"Cuant de Orion lus
Tres reys la stralla veran,
Deo omnipotent
Adora lo vingaran.
Un present inferan
De mil encens y or,
A lu benuit seño,
Que conesce cual se vol.
    Disciarem lu dol, etc.

"Tot fu gayant
Para cumplé la prumas,
Y lu Esperit sant
De un angel fau gramas,
Gran foc ences,
Que crama lu curagia.
Damos da lenguagia
Para fe lo que Deo vol.
    Disciarem lu dol, etc.

"Cuant trespasá
De quest mon nostra Señora,
Al cel s' empugia.
Sun fil la matescia ora,
O, Emperadora!

"In Bethlehem,
In the Holy Land,
Was born the Saviour,
With great joy;
The little child
Who all the world would save,
Which no one could accomplish
But God alone.
    CHORUS.

"When in the East
Three kings the star did see,
God omnipotent
To adore they came.
A present they made him
Of myrrh and gold,
To the blessed Saviour,
Who knows every one.
    CHORUS.

"All burning with zeal
To accomplish the promises,
The Holy Spirit
From an angel was sent forth.
A great fire was kindled,
And courage inflamed him.
God give us language
To do thy will.
    CHORUS.

"When we have passed
From this world, our Lady,
To heaven we are raised.
Your Son, at the same hour,
O Queen,

Que del cel san eligida,	Who art of Heaven the choicest
Lu rosa florida,	Blooming rose!
Mé resplenden que un sol.	More brilliant than the sun.
Disciarem lu dol, etc.	CHORUS.
"Y el tercer groin	On the third day
Que Jesus resunta,	Our Jesus arose,
Deo y aboroma,	The celestial God
Que la mort triumfa.	Over death triumphant.
De alli se ballá	From hence he has gone
Para perldra Lucife	To overcome Satan
An tot a sen pendá,	Throughout the whole world.
Que de nostro ser al sol.	Our protector and guide.
Disciarem lu dol," etc.	CHORUS.

After this hymn the following stanzas, soliciting the customary gifts of cakes or eggs, are sung:

* * * * *   * * * * *

"Lu cet gois vam cantant,	"These seven stanzas sung,
Regina celestial.	Celestial queen
Damos pan y alagria!	Give us peace and joy!
Yabonas festas tingan;	May you enjoy a good feast;
Y vos da sus bonas festas,	We wish a happy time,
Damos dinés de sus nous,	Give us of your bounty.
Sempre tarem lus neans Uestas	We always have our hands ready
Para recibi un grapat de nes.	Thy bounty to receive.
Y, el giorn de pascua florida	Let us now the Easter feast
Alagramos y, giuntament.	Together enjoy.
As qui es mort par dar nos vida;	He died to save us;
Y via glorosiamente,	Let us be joyful.
A questa casa está empedrada,	This house is walled round,
Bien halla que la empedro.	Blessed be he who walled it about.
San amo de aquesta casa	The owner of this house
Baldria duná un do,	Ought to give us a token,

Formagiada o empanada.	Either a cake or a tart.
Cucutta a flao,	We like anything,
Cual se val casa sue grada,	So you say not no."
Sol que no rue digas que no."	* * * * *

The shutters are then opened by the people within, and a supply of cakes or other pastry is dropped into a bag carried by one of the party, who acknowledge the gift in the following lines, and then depart:

" Aquesta casa reta empedrada,	" This house is walled round,
Empedrada de cuastro vens,	Walled round on four sides.
Sun amo de aquesta casa,	The owner of this house
Es omo de compliment."	Is a polite gentleman."

If nothing is given, the last line reads thus:

" No es homo de compliment."	" Is not a polite gentleman."

This song is repeated throughout the city until midnight. To the listener it has a peculiar fascination like some of the tunes from popular operas, keeping one awake to listen to its strains, even after many repetitions have rendered the singing monotonous.

The walls of the United States barracks are probably the oldest structures in the place. An old house on Hospital Street, torn down in 1871, when Mr. Pendleton built a very pretty cottage upon the same ground, was said by old residents to have been the oldest house in the town. The former residence of the attorney-general during the English possession stood just south of the Worth House on the corner of Bay and Green Streets. This was a very old structure, though built in too costly a manner to have been one of the earliest buildings, one of which in English times still bore the date 1571. The house was built by a Spaniard named Ysnada. Its beams were made of a wood brought from Cuba, which resembled our royal palm in being susceptible of taking a high polish. The staircases, wainscoting, and panels were of lignum-vitæ. For many years the house stood in too dilapidated a condition for occupancy. Finally the wood was torn out by curiosity hunters and dealers, and made into canes and other mementoes of "the oldest house in St. Augustine."

The present sea-wall was built between 1835 and 1843, under the superintendence of Colonel Dancey, now living at his orange grove called Buena Vista, on the St. Johns River. He was then a captain in the U. S. Army. The wall is ten feet above low-water mark, seven feet thick at the base, and three feet wide on top, capped with granite, and extends along the whole front of the city, from the old fort on the north to the barracks on the south, about three-quarters of a mile in length. Opposite the plaza the wall forms a basin for small boats. Under Colonel Dancey the government spent three appropriations of fifty thousand dollars each, having spent twenty thousand dollars previously in preparation for the work. Captain Benham spent two appropriations of fifty thousand dollars each in covering the wall with granite slabs, as it was found that the coquina was rapidly wearing away under the tread of pedestrians using the wall as a promenade. Much of the pleasure of this otherwise delightful promenade is marred by the narrowness of the curbing, making the passing difficult. This feature is said to be unobjectionable to lovers, who are credited with the opinion that to see St. Augustine aright it is necessary to promenade the sea-wall by moonlight, viewing the rippling waters of the bay, with the roar of the surf on the neighboring beach as an interlude to the sweeter music of their own voices. Colonel Dancey built the present causeway leading to the depot in 1837 at the expense of the United States. His successor, Captain Benham, superintended the construction of the water battery at the fort, and other repairs made to the property of the United States within the city.

Under the dominion of the United States, St. Augustine soon became a health and pleasure resort. Without manufactures, with, as yet, no products of agriculture for export, its fine port is destitute of commerce, and its easy-going population have ever since depended upon the attractions offered by their city to invalids and persons of fortune, for the means with which to procure the necessaries and luxuries which its inhabitants enjoy in a fair measure. Strangers often wonder how the town is supported, but upon investigation it is found that the frugality of the people is remarkable. Their independence comes from what they save rather than from what they earn. While there is little wealth among its citizens, there is little actual want. The many girls and young ladies always dress with neatness and taste, and many earn the means to support themselves by braiding palmetto for hats and baskets, making feather flowers, shell, and fish-scale ornaments, and bouquets of the native grasses. The town has long been noted for the number and health of its young children.

In 1834 the city contained 1,739 inhabitants, of whom 498 were males, 519 females, 151 free colored persons, and 571 slaves. Of these, 10 were lawyers, 3 doctors, 1 printer, 7 dry-goods dealers, 6 keepers of boarding-houses, 13 grocers, 1 painter, 7 carpenters, 4 masons, 2 blacksmiths, 1 gunsmith, 2 shoemakers, 1 baker, 2 tailors, 1 tanner, and 5 cigar-makers. The present population of the city is, by the census of 1880, about 2,300, of which about the same number follow the above callings as in 1834, with the exception of lawyers and grocers, of whom there are not more than half the former number. There is no bank in the city, its place being supplied by the money-order department of the post-office. The colored population are much more intelligent, better educated, and generally superior to the individuals of that unfortunate race found in other parts of the South. This is partly owing to the large number of free negroes here before the Emancipation, and also to the advantages they have derived from contact with the visitors and residents coming from all parts of the country. In 1843 the poet Bryant remarked the fact above stated, saying, "In the colored people whom I saw in the Catholic church I remarked a more agreeable, open, and gentle physiognomy than I have been accustomed to see in that class." *

Many of the most interesting old structures have, unfortunately, been torn down. As these attractive old relics of antiquity are swept away, some ignorant iconoclast bids the people rejoice over a new "city improvement," forgetting that there are many modern cities in America, and but one "ancient city." The building now used as a post-office has, in this way, been remodeled from a quaint and interesting old Spanish structure, with its court-yard and balconies, into a commonplace modern structure. Even the old coquina lunette standing in the same yard on the corner of King and Tolomato Streets had to succumb to personal interest and the demand for "improvements," and was swept away, thus depriving the city of one of its most attractive mementoes.

The fort, the Spanish monument, the cathedral, and the city

---

* Fairbanks's History, p. 197.

gates yet remain, preserved from the hands of vandals. The city has lately repaired the sentry-boxes, constructed in the pilasters of the city gate, and doubtless from this time on there will be an effort made to preserve all of the old relics yet remaining.

In 1879 the Ladies' Memorial Association obtained permission of the city to remove to the plaza a monument that had been erected on St. George Street to the memory of the soldiers of St. Augustine and vicinity who died in the late "war between the States." This monument now stands near the east end of the plaza, and preserves the names of those whose memory it is intended to perpetuate, engraved upon two marble slabs set into the masonry. Its inscriptions are as follows :

"Our dead."

"Erected by the Ladies' Memorial Association of St. Augustine, Fla., A.D. 1872."

"In Memoriam. Our loved ones who gave their lives in the service of the Confederate States."

In the military cemetery near the barracks are three small pyramids built of masonry and whitewashed, marking the place where are interred the remains of Major Dade and his one hundred and seven comrades massacred by the Indians near the Withlacoochee River, on the 28th of December, 1835. They were buried on the battle-field by a detachment that was sent out for their succor, but arrived too late. Upon the removal of their remains to St. Augustine, these pyramids were erected, and also a handsome monument. The monument is of marble, a broken pillar or shaft upon a square pedestal, with inscriptions on the four faces.

On the first we read:

"This monument, in token of respectful and affectionate remembrance by their comrades of all grades, is committed to the care and preservation of the garrison of St. Augustine."

On another the following:

"A mute record of all the officers who perished, and are here and elsewhere deposited, as also a portion of the soldiers, has been prepared and placed in the office of the adjutant of the post, where it is hoped it will be carefully and perpetually preserved."

On another:

"The conflict in which so many perished in battle, and by disease, commenced 25th December, 1835, and terminated 14th August, 1842."

On the last:

"Sacred to the memory of the officers and soldiers killed in battle and died in service during the Florida War."

Near this cemetery is the post hospital, a convenient and airy building. A large building on St. George Street, erected in 1874, is occupied by the society of nuns called Sisters of St. Joseph. Many of the female children of the city are taught by the sisters in this building, and children from abroad are also received, and lodge in the building. The nuns of St. Augustine have always had the reputation of making fine lace-work, and much of their work is purchased by visitors.

A large and comfortable building was erected a few years since as a home for aged and infirm colored persons. It stands back from King Street just west of Santa Maria Creek. Doctor Bronson and Mr. Buckingham Smith were chiefly instrumental in erecting the building and furnishing the endowment, which is managed by a board of trustees. The general management of the Home and its inmates is given to a matron chosen by the ladies of the different church parishes, subject to the approval of the board of trustees.

The wooden building upon a circular foundation of coquina standing in the bay north of the basin is the bath-house. In the winter it is kept heated, and warm salt-water baths are furnished to visitors. During the summer it is liberally patronized for swimming baths by the citizens of the place and many summer visitors, who come from the interior of the State to spend the hot months at the seaside. Probably a larger proportion of the ladies of St. Augustine know how to swim than of any other place in the country.

Within the last few years there have been a number of handsome houses built in the city by wealthy gentlemen who occupy them during the winter season. Mr. H. P. Kingsland of New York has a fine residence north of the gates upon the shell road. This is probably the most expensive of the houses built by non-residents, though the fine house built by the late Hy. Ball upon his estate on Tolomato Street is said to have cost a large sum of money. The grounds and orange grove on this place were very attractive during the life of Mr. Ball, and it is a place much frequented by visitors.

Mr. Geo. L. Lorillard has lately purchased the "Stone" mansion on St. George Street, and is ornamenting the grounds, and otherwise making the place more attractive.

Mr. Tyler, Mr. Ammidown, Mr. Howard, Mr. Bronson, Mr. Alexander, and Mr. Wilson each have fine residences on St. George Street south of the plaza. Mr. Edgar has a handsome coquina house on the bay, while the residence of ex-Senator Gilbert on the south, and the residence and orange grove of Dr. Anderson on the north, are sure to attract the notice of the stranger entering the city from the causeway. All of these residences have attractive grounds, ornamentally laid out, and artistically adorned, containing a great variety of most beautiful roses and ornamental plants and flowers. The roses especially are congenial to the soil and climate, and are in the early winter months most attractive in their wealth of bloom. This shrub in some of its varieties, here attains the proportions of a tree. The rose tree in the garden of Mr. Oliveros was fifteen feet high, rising from a stock twenty-one inches in circumference, and its branches covered a space eighteen feet in diameter. The tree is dead, but the stump is still to be seen.

The shell road extends for about a mile north of the city, and is much used during the winter season. Carriages, buggies, and saddle-horses for hire are usually standing at all hours in front of the hotels or near the plaza, and on fair days are well patronized. Mr. Williams and Mr. Hildreth, north of the city, have attractive places which are much visited by tourists. When the tide is low there is a short but quite hard drive along the edge of the St. Sebastian River. There is an interesting drive to a suburb west of the city called Ravenswood, where is a spring called from the famous Ponce de Leon. A great natural curiosity is a large spring in the ocean about three miles off the coast near Matanzas Inlet, eighteen miles south of St. Augustine. This spring has been described in the publications of the U. S. Coast Survey. There is a comfortable hotel kept by Mr. Darius Allen at Matanzas, which is often filled with hunting and fishing parties. The house stands on the narrow sand reef between the Matanzas River and the ocean.

At the outbreak of the war of the Rebellion the Union sentiment, which existed among a considerable portion of the community, was stifled by the taunts of cowardice and the popular frenzy for secession. A number of the inhabitants, being unable to make their influence felt at the election of delegates, prepared and had presented to the convention that passed the ordinance of secession a letter of protest against such a course. The only effect of this letter was to place the signers in such a position that they were advised to volunteer at once to serve in the Confederate army.

In March, 1862, the United States forces took possession of the town, which they held until the close of the war. The city was taken by a naval force under command of Lieut. S. F. Du Pont, afterward Admiral Du Pont.

In his report to the Secretary of the Navy, Flag-Officer Du Pont speaks of the occupation of the place in a tone exhibiting less of exultation than sadness, that a place which had enjoyed so many favors at the hands of the government should have taken part in an attempt at its overthrow.

It is perhaps too soon after the close of the struggle to discuss the events of that period. As a matter of history, however, I give the report of Commander Rodgers, who received the surrender of the town. In transmitting the report, Flag-Officer Du Pont adds: "The American flag is flying once more over that old city, raised by the hands of its own people."

The following is Commander Rodgers's report:

"UNITED STATES FLAG-SHIP WABASH,
"OFF ST. AUGUSTINE, FLORIDA, *March* 12, 1862.

"SIR: Having crossed the bar with some difficulty, in obedience to your orders, I approached St. Augustine under a flag of truce, and as I drew near the city a white flag was hoisted upon one of the bastions of Fort Marion.

"Landing at the wharf and inquiring for the chief authorities I was soon joined by the mayor, and conducted to the City Hall, where the municipal authorities were assembled.

"I informed them that having come to restore the authority of the United States, you had deemed it more kind to send an unarmed boat to inform the citizens of your determination than to occupy the town at once by force of arms; that you were desirous to calm any apprehension of harsh treatment that might exist in their minds, and that you should carefully respect the persons and property of all citizens who submitted to the authority of the United States; that you had a single purpose—to restore the state of affairs which existed before the Rebellion. I informed the municipal authorities that so long as they respected the authority of the government we serve, and acted in good faith, municipal affairs would be left in their own hands, so far as might be consistent with the exigencies of the times.

"The mayor and council then informed me that the place had been evacuated the preceding night by two companies of Florida troops, and that they gladly received the assurance I gave them, and placed the city in my hands. I recommended them to hoist the flag of the Union at once, and in prompt accordance with the advice, by order of the mayor the national ensign was displayed from the flagstaff of the fort. * * * *

"I called upon the clergymen of the city requesting them to reassure the people, and to confide in our kind intentions toward them.

"About fifteen hundred people remain in St. Augustine, about

8*

one-fifth of the inhabitants having fled. I believe that there are many citizens who are earnestly attached to the Union, a large number who are silently opposed to it, and a still larger number who care very little about the matter.

"I think that nearly all of the men acquiesce in the condition of affairs we are now establishing.

"There is much violent and pestilent feeling among the women. They seem to mistake treason for courage, and have a theatrical desire to figure as heroines. Their minds have doubtless been filled with the falsehoods so industriously circulated in regard to the lust and hatred of our troops. On the night before our arrival, a party of women assembled in front of the barracks and cut down the flag-staff, in order that it might not be used to support the old flag. The men seemed anxious to conciliate in every way. There is a great scarcity of provisions in the place. There seems to be no money, except the wretched paper currency of the Rebellion, and much poverty exists. In the water-battery at the fort are three fine army thirty-two-pounders, of 7,000 pounds, and two eight-inch seacoast howitzers, of 5,600 pounds, with shot and some powder. There are a number of very old guns in the fort, useless and not mounted.

* * * * * * * * * * *

"I have the honor to be very respectfully,

"C. R. P. RODGERS, *Commander.*

"*Flag Officer*, S. F. Du Pont,

"Commanding S. Atlantic Blockading Station."

Mr. Christobal Bravo, an old and much-respected citizen of the place, who is still alive, was the mayor who surrendered the town.

Immediately after the close of the Rebellion, real estate in the city possessed very little value. Within a short time, however, as a few wealthy men began to secure sites for winter residences, the prices suddenly leaped to the full value, and, in many cases, fictitious values, which they have since maintained.

The climate of St. Augustine is unsurpassed by that of any location in the world. The mass of testimony to its healthfulness and agreeableness is constantly accumulating, and dates from its first settlement.

The extreme old age attained by the aborigines in Florida has been referred to in the extract from Laudonnère. Romans mentions a man, eighty-five years old, who had gone five miles on foot to catch fish, while his mother was meantime busy preparing bread.

The following quaint testimony is from "Romans's History":

"Before I quit this subject of the air, I cannot help taking notice of a remark, which I have read somewhere, made by Dr. James McKenzie, which is, 'The soon molding of the bread, moistness of sponge, dissolution of loaf sugar, and rusting of metals,' are marks of a bad air.' Now every one of those marks are more to be seen at St. Augustine than in any place I ever was at. And yet I do not think that on all the continent there is a more healthy spot. Burials have been less frequent here than anywhere else, where an equal number of inhabitants are found; and it was remarked, during my stay there, that, when a detachment of the royal regiment of artillery once arrived there in a sickly state, none of the inhabitants caught the contagion, and the troops themselves soon recruited. The Spanish inhabitants lived here to a great age, and certain it is, that the people of the Havannah looked on it as their Montpellier, frequenting it for the sake of health."

Forbes remarks that the Ninth Regiment of British troops never lost a man by natural death during the eight months they were quartered in the town. The undeviating salubrity "of St. Augustine, under the British flag, was certainly augmented by the perfect cleanliness and neatness which was the characteristic of the town during that epoch, and that it continued so while the buildings crumbled into ruins over the heads of the indolent Spaniards, and the dirt and nuisance augmented in every lot is an additional proof of the natural healthfulness of the place." *

From October to June the weather is temperate, the thermometer having a mean of fifty-eight degrees in the winter, and sixty-eight degrees in the spring. During the winter months there are frequent cloudy days, and usually several cold storms in a season. From twenty-five years' observations Dr. Baldwin, of Jacksonville, prepared a table showing the average of clear days in January to be $20\frac{8}{10}$; February, $19\frac{5}{10}$; March, $20\frac{4}{10}$; April, 25. For the whole year, 235 clear days.

The climate of St. Augustine is sufficiently cold in winter to brace up the constitution, after being relaxed by summer heats. On the other hand, it is sufficiently warm to entice the invalid to be out of doors, and to present opportunities for open-air exercises. The east winds that prevail are tempered by the proximity of the Gulf Stream, a vast volume of warm water moving along the coast of Florida, whose effect is felt thousands of miles farther north in modifying the temperature of the British Isles.

The peculiar location of St. Augustine, upon a narrow peninsula, provides a natural drainage that renders the place particularly desirable as a health resort. Through the winter rains are

---

* Forbes's Sketches.

infrequent, that being the dry season in Florida ; whatever rain falls, however, is immediately absorbed by the sandy soil, and, in many parts of the city, the slope of the surface carries the rain-fall immediately into the tide-water environing the city, before it has time to be absorbed by the earth.

The mean relative humidity for the five winter months of several localities, recommended as health resorts, is shown in a table compiled by C. J. Kenworthy, M.D., of Jacksonville, Fla., and published by him in his work on "The Climatology of Florida." I take the liberty of using his data. The humidity of St. Augustine during the winter months is nearly the same as that of Jacksonville. At Mentone and Cannes the mean relative humidity for the five months, beginning in November, is.. $72\frac{4}{10}$ per cent.

Breckenridge, Minn.....................	$79\frac{6}{10}$ "
Bismark, Dak....;.....................	$76\frac{5}{10}$ "
Nassau, N. P..........................	$73\frac{2}{10}$ "
Punta Rassa, Fla. (on the Gulf coast)......	$72\frac{7}{10}$ "
Jacksonville, "	$68\frac{8}{10}$ "

Thus it will be seen that, although we sometimes have fogs and cloudy weather, the humidity of the atmosphere is less than that of several noted health resorts, some of which are at a considerable elevation. Finally, the medical attendance and supply of nourishing and appetizing food available at St. Augustine are all that could be desired. The hotels and boarding-houses are excellent; while the opportunities and inducements for open-air recreations and exercises are superior.

With the close connections furnished by the lines of railway lately completed to Jacksonville, that city will doubtless become the objective point of the Florida-bound tourist. At that place time-tables can be obtained of the river steamers and the railway from Tocoi, on the St. Johns River, to St. Augustine; and, by correspondence, accommodations can be secured in advance, during the season, when the hotels and boarding-houses of St. Augustine are likely to be crowded.

All visitors to Florida, and especially those who come for recreation, should be sure to spend a portion of the season, at least, in St. Augustine.

www.ingramcontent.com/pod-product-compliance
Lightning Source LLC
Chambersburg PA
CBHW032025230426
43671CB00005B/207